I0014666

The Vibe Coding Playbook

Your Guide to AI-Powered Programming

HARRELL HOWARD

Table of Contents

Introduction: Redefining Programming

Programming has changed. What once required memorizing syntax and writing every line by hand now flows from simple human instructions. This shift marks a fundamental change in how we create software.

Picture this: You sit at your computer, describe what you want to build, and watch as code appears before your eyes. This isn't science fiction—it's the reality of coding with AI assistance. The days of staring at a blank editor, struggling to remember exact function names or syntax rules, are fading into history.

Vibe coding represents this new approach to programming. Rather than focusing on the mechanics of code, you concentrate on your intent—what you want to accomplish. The AI handles the translation from your ideas into functional code. This book explores this revolutionary approach to software creation.

The Shift From Manual Coding to Intent-Driven Workflows

Traditional programming required developers to manually write every character of code. Each semicolon, bracket, and variable name needed careful placement. Learning to code meant memorizing rules, syntax, and libraries—a process that took years to master.

AI-powered programming flips this model. Now, you express your goals in plain language, and AI tools generate the corresponding code. This approach removes many technical barriers that previously kept programming exclusive to those willing to invest significant time learning syntax.

Consider building a simple web application. In the past, you'd need to:

- Learn HTML, CSS, and JavaScript
- Understand DOM manipulation
- Master event handling
- Write code for each component manually

With vibe coding, you might simply say: "Create a webpage with a form that collects user email addresses and stores them in a database." The AI generates the necessary code structure, which you can then review and refine.

This shift doesn't eliminate the need for programming knowledge. Rather, it changes what kind of knowledge matters most. Understanding programming concepts, patterns, and best practices becomes more valuable than memorizing syntax details.

What Vibe Coding Means in Practice

Vibe coding isn't just about generating code through prompts. It represents a holistic approach to programming that includes:

Collaborative Creation: You and AI tools work together, with each bringing different strengths to the process. The AI handles routine coding tasks while you provide direction, creativity, and quality control.

Rapid Prototyping: Ideas transform into working code quickly. This speed allows you to test concepts, gather feedback, and iterate faster than ever before.

Focus on Problem-Solving: With less time spent on syntax and boilerplate code, you can dedicate more attention to solving the core problems your software addresses.

Accessible Development: Programming becomes more accessible to people without formal training. Someone with domain expertise but limited coding experience can now create functional software.

Continuous Learning: Both you and the AI improve over time. As you learn to communicate more effectively with AI tools, they learn to better understand your preferences and patterns.

In practice, vibe coding often looks like a conversation. You might start with a general request, review what the AI produces, ask for changes, and gradually refine the output until it meets your needs. This iterative process feels more natural than traditional programming for many people.

The Role of AI Tools in Simplifying Software Creation

AI coding assistants serve multiple roles in the development process:

Code Generation: Creating new code based on your descriptions or completing partial code you've started.

Documentation: Explaining existing code, generating comments, or creating documentation for APIs and functions.

Debugging: Identifying potential issues in your code and suggesting fixes.

Refactoring: Restructuring existing code to improve its quality without changing its behavior.

Learning Resources: Providing explanations and examples to help you understand programming concepts.

Tools like GitHub Copilot integrate directly into your code editor, offering suggestions as you type. Others, like ChatGPT, provide a conversational interface where you can discuss your programming needs. Specialized tools focus on specific languages or frameworks, offering deeper expertise in particular domains.

These tools don't replace human developers—they amplify their capabilities. An experienced developer using AI tools can work faster and tackle more complex projects. A beginner can create working software that would have been beyond their reach without assistance.

Why This Approach is Changing Traditional Development Dynamics

The rise of vibe coding is reshaping software development in several ways:

Skill Valuation: The skills most valued in developers are evolving. The ability to effectively communicate with AI tools, review generated code, and integrate components becomes more important than writing code from scratch.

Project Timelines: Development cycles compress as many routine tasks accelerate. Projects that once took months might now complete in weeks.

Team Composition: Development teams may include more non-traditional programmers—domain experts who use AI tools to implement their ideas without needing to become full-fledged developers.

Learning Curves: The path to becoming productive as a developer is changing. Newcomers can start creating useful software much earlier in their learning journey.

Code Ownership: Questions arise about who "wrote" the code—the developer who prompted the

AI, the AI system itself, or the developers whose work trained the AI model.

These changes bring both opportunities and challenges. Organizations that embrace AI-assisted development gain efficiency and can involve more team members in the coding process. At the same time, they must address questions about code quality, security, and the evolving role of human developers.

The shift toward vibe coding doesn't mean programming is becoming less skilled—it means the skills are changing. The most successful developers will be those who adapt to this new paradigm, learning to work with AI tools as partners rather than seeing them as threats or mere utilities.

As we explore the chapters ahead, you'll learn practical techniques for vibe coding, discover how to overcome common challenges, and develop strategies for creating high-quality software in this new era of AI-assisted development.

The future of programming isn't about humans being replaced by AI—it's about humans and AI working together to create better software than either could produce alone. Welcome to the world of vibe coding.

Chapter 1: Foundations of Vibe Coding

The world of programming has undergone a quiet revolution. Where developers once typed every character by hand, they now collaborate with artificial intelligence to bring ideas to life. This shift represents more than just a new tool—it's a fundamental change in how we approach software creation.

Vibe coding sits at the heart of this transformation. But what exactly makes this approach different, and how do these AI systems actually work? Let's explore the foundations that make this new programming paradigm possible.

How AI Coding Assistants Work

AI coding assistants might seem magical at first glance, but they operate on understandable principles. These systems rely on large language models (LLMs) trained on vast collections of code and text. Through this training, they learn patterns in programming languages, common solutions to problems, and the relationship between human language and code.

When you interact with an AI coding assistant, several processes happen behind the scenes:

Pattern Recognition: The AI identifies patterns in your request that match patterns it learned during training. If you ask for "a function that sorts a list of numbers," it recognizes this as a common programming task.

Context Analysis: The system examines any existing code you've provided, your previous interactions, and other contextual clues to understand what you're trying to accomplish.

Code Generation: Based on its training and your input, the AI produces code that attempts to fulfill your request. This generation isn't random—it follows the statistical patterns the system learned from millions of code examples.

Feedback Integration: As you provide feedback on the generated code, the system refines its understanding of your needs and adjusts its outputs accordingly.

These systems don't "understand" code in the way human programmers do. They don't reason about algorithms or debug logical errors through conscious thought. Instead, they recognize patterns and generate statistically likely responses based on their training.

This distinction matters because it helps explain both the strengths and limitations of AI coding assistants. They excel at producing code that follows common patterns but may struggle with novel approaches or complex logical reasoning.

Predictive Modeling and Contextual Code Generation

The core technology behind AI coding assistants is predictive modeling. These systems predict what code should come next based on what came before—similar to how your phone predicts the next word you might type.

For code generation, this prediction happens at multiple levels:

Token Level: Predicting the next character, keyword, or symbol
Line Level: Generating complete lines of code
Block Level: Creating entire functions or classes
File Level: Producing complete program files

The quality of these predictions depends heavily on context. The more relevant context you provide, the better the AI can tailor its output to your needs. This context might include:

- Your description of what you want to accomplish
- Code you've already written
- Comments explaining your intent
- Examples of similar code
- Specifications for the desired behavior

Contextual code generation works best when you communicate clearly with the AI. Vague requests like "write some code" yield generic results, while specific requests like "create a Python function that calculates the Fibonacci sequence using recursion" produce more targeted outputs.

This contextual nature makes AI coding assistants particularly valuable for tasks where you know what you want but might not remember the exact syntax or implementation details. The AI fills in these gaps based on its training.

Tools Like GitHub Copilot, Cursor, and ChatGPT in Action

Several AI tools have emerged to support vibe coding, each with unique strengths:

GitHub Copilot integrates directly into your code editor, offering suggestions as you type. It excels at completing lines and functions based on comments and existing code. Copilot feels like a pair programmer watching over your shoulder, ready to suggest the next few lines whenever you pause.

A developer might write a comment like:

Function to calculate the area of a circle given its radius

And Copilot might suggest:

```
def calculate_circle_area(radius):
    return 3.14159 * radius * radius
```

Cursor takes this concept further by combining a code editor with AI capabilities. Beyond code completion, it helps with explaining code, refactoring, and generating entire functions based on natural language descriptions. Cursor aims to be a comprehensive development environment built around AI assistance.

ChatGPT offers a conversational interface for coding help. Rather than integrating into your editor, it provides a space where you can discuss programming problems, request code samples, or ask for explanations. This conversational approach allows for more complex requests and iterative refinement.

A typical ChatGPT interaction might look like:

User: "How would I create a simple web server in Node.js that returns 'Hello World'?"

ChatGPT: *[Provides code for a basic Node.js server]*

User: "Can you modify that to read the message from an environment variable?"

ChatGPT: *[Provides updated code incorporating the request]*

These tools represent different approaches to the same goal: making programming more accessible and efficient through AI assistance. The best choice depends on your workflow, preferences, and specific needs.

The Intent-Driven Mindset: Speaking Code Through Prompts

Vibe coding requires a shift in mindset from traditional programming. Rather than thinking about how to implement a solution, you focus on what you want to accomplish. This intent-driven approach changes how you communicate with your development tools.

Effective prompting—the art of communicating with AI systems—becomes a crucial skill. Good prompts for coding assistants typically include:

Clear Objectives: What should the code accomplish?
Constraints: Any limitations or requirements the solution must meet
Context: Relevant information about the larger project or environment
Examples: Sample inputs and expected outputs
Preferences: Coding style, language features, or approaches you prefer

Learning to craft effective prompts takes practice. You'll likely start with simple requests and gradually develop the ability to communicate more complex intentions.

This shift toward intent-driven programming doesn't mean abandoning technical knowledge. Rather, it changes how you apply that knowledge. Instead of using your expertise to write every line of code, you use it to:

- Formulate clear requests
- Evaluate generated code
- Identify potential issues
- Guide the AI toward better solutions
- Integrate generated components into larger systems

The most successful vibe coders develop a collaborative relationship with AI tools. They learn what kinds of requests produce the best results and how to iteratively refine both their prompts and the generated code.

Understanding the Limits of AI-Generated Code

While AI coding assistants offer remarkable capabilities, they come with important limitations:

Training Data Boundaries: AI can only generate code based on patterns in its training data. Novel approaches or very recent technologies may be outside its knowledge.

Logical Reasoning: These systems don't truly "understand" logic or causality. They may produce code that looks correct but contains subtle logical errors.

Security Awareness: AI tools might generate code with security vulnerabilities if not specifically prompted to consider security implications.

Optimization Knowledge: Generated code often works but isn't optimized for performance, memory usage, or other efficiency metrics.

Domain Expertise: AI lacks deep understanding of specific business domains or specialized fields unless explicitly guided.

Contextual Limitations: Most systems have limits on how much context they can consider at once, making it challenging to understand very large codebases.

These limitations don't diminish the value of AI coding assistants, but they highlight the continued importance of human judgment. The most effective approach combines AI's ability to generate code quickly with human expertise in evaluating and refining that code.

Recognizing these boundaries helps set realistic expectations. AI coding assistants are powerful tools that can dramatically increase your productivity, but they're not magical solutions that eliminate the need for programming knowledge.

The relationship between developer and AI is evolving rapidly. As these tools improve, some current limitations will fade while new capabilities emerge. Staying aware of both the strengths and weaknesses of AI-generated code allows you to use these tools responsibly and effectively.

In the next chapter, we'll explore how to set up your workspace for AI-assisted development and take your first steps with vibe coding. You'll learn practical techniques for getting started with these tools and integrating them into your development workflow.

Chapter 2: Getting Started with Vibe Coding

Starting your journey with AI-assisted programming might feel like stepping into unfamiliar territory. The good news? This path is more accessible than traditional coding approaches. Let's walk through how to set up your environment, choose the right tools, and begin creating with AI assistance.

Setting Up Your Workspace for AI-Assisted Development

Your workspace forms the foundation of your vibe coding experience. A well-organized environment helps you communicate effectively with AI tools and integrate their suggestions into your projects.

Choose a Compatible Code Editor

Many AI coding assistants integrate directly with popular code editors. Some options include:

- Visual Studio Code with GitHub Copilot extension
- Cursor (built with AI assistance in mind)
- JetBrains IDEs (IntelliJ, PyCharm, WebStorm) with AI plugins

- Neovim with coding assistant extensions

Your editor should feel comfortable and match your workflow preferences. The best choice balances familiarity with AI integration capabilities.

Set Up Version Control

Version control becomes even more important when working with AI-generated code. Set up Git repositories for your projects to:

- Track changes between AI suggestions and your modifications
- Revert to previous versions if needed
- Document the evolution of your code through commit messages

This practice creates a safety net as you experiment with AI-generated solutions.

Create a Prompt Library

Start a document or note file for storing effective prompts. As you discover phrasings that produce good results, save them for future use. Your prompt library might include:

- Template requests for common coding tasks

- Phrases that help clarify your intent
- Examples of prompts that yielded particularly good results

This resource will grow more valuable as you gain experience with vibe coding.

Organize Reference Materials

Keep documentation for your programming languages, frameworks, and libraries easily accessible. AI tools might generate code using features you're unfamiliar with, and having references handy helps you understand these suggestions.

Consider Computational Resources

Some AI coding tools run locally on your machine, while others operate in the cloud. Local tools offer privacy but require more powerful hardware. Cloud-based options work on almost any computer but require internet connectivity and may raise privacy considerations for sensitive projects.

Choosing the Right Tools for Your Project

The growing ecosystem of AI coding assistants offers options for various needs and preferences. Consider these factors when selecting tools:

Project Type and Scale

Different tools excel at different types of projects:

- For small scripts or isolated functions, almost any AI coding assistant will work well
- For web development, tools with strong JavaScript, HTML, and CSS capabilities shine
- For data science, look for tools with Python expertise and knowledge of relevant libraries
- For large applications, consider tools that can understand broader context and project structure

Integration Requirements

How will the AI tool fit into your existing workflow?

- Editor plugins maintain your current environment while adding AI capabilities
- Standalone AI chat interfaces offer flexibility but require copying code between applications

- Specialized AI-first editors provide tight integration but may require adapting to a new environment

Learning Curve

Some tools require learning specific prompting techniques or commands:

- GitHub Copilot works almost invisibly, suggesting code as you type
- ChatGPT requires learning conversational prompting strategies
- Specialized coding assistants might have unique syntax for requests

Cost Considerations

AI coding tools range from free to subscription-based:

- Free options often have usage limits or reduced capabilities
- Paid tools typically offer more features and higher usage limits
- Some tools offer free tiers for individual developers and paid plans for teams

Privacy and Security

If you work with sensitive code or proprietary information:

- Check whether the tool sends your code to external servers
- Review the provider's data usage and retention policies
- Consider locally-running options for highly sensitive projects

For beginners, starting with a general-purpose tool like GitHub Copilot or ChatGPT provides a good introduction to vibe coding. As you gain experience, you might add specialized tools for specific aspects of your workflow.

Writing Effective Prompts: Communicating with AI

The art of prompting—clearly communicating your intent to AI systems—stands as perhaps the most important skill in vibe coding. Well-crafted prompts lead to better code suggestions and fewer iterations.

Be Specific About Your Goal

Compare these two prompts:

Vague: "Write a function to process data."
Specific: "Write a Python function that takes a CSV file path as input, reads the file, filters rows where the 'Status' column equals 'Active', and returns a list of dictionaries containing only the 'ID' and 'Name' columns."

The specific prompt provides clear guidance about inputs, processing steps, and expected outputs.

Include Context and Constraints

Help the AI understand the bigger picture:

"This function will be part of a Flask web application. It needs to handle large files efficiently and should raise appropriate exceptions if the file is missing or malformed. The function should follow PEP 8 style guidelines."

This additional information helps the AI generate code that fits your specific situation.

Use Examples

Examples clarify your expectations:

"For instance, if the CSV contains:

```
ID,Name,Status,Date
1,Alice,Active,2023-01-01
2,Bob,Inactive,2023-01-02
3,Charlie,Active,2023-01-03
```

The function should return:

```
[
    {"ID": "1", "Name": "Alice"},
    {"ID": "3", "Name": "Charlie"}
]
```
"

Examples reduce ambiguity and help the AI understand exactly what you want.

Request Explanations

Ask the AI to explain its code:

"Please add comments explaining any complex parts of the code and why you made specific implementation choices."

This helps you understand the generated code and learn from the AI's approach.

Iterate and Refine

Treat prompting as a conversation:

1. Start with a basic request
2. Review the generated code
3. Ask for specific modifications or improvements
4. Continue refining until satisfied

Each iteration helps the AI better understand your needs.

Learn From Successful Prompts

When you receive particularly good results, analyze what made your prompt effective. Was it the level of detail? The examples you provided? The specific terminology you used? Apply these insights to future prompts.

Expectations for Beginners: What AI Can and Cannot Do

Setting realistic expectations helps avoid frustration as you begin your vibe coding journey.

What AI Coding Assistants Can Do Well:

Generate Boilerplate Code: AI excels at creating standard structures like class definitions, API endpoints, or configuration files.

Implement Common Patterns: For well-established programming patterns, AI can generate solid implementations.

Suggest Completions: As you write code, AI can offer logical next steps or completions.

Explain Existing Code: AI can help you understand unfamiliar code by explaining what it does.

Convert Between Languages: Need to rewrite a Python function in JavaScript? AI can help with these translations.

What AI Coding Assistants Struggle With:

Novel Algorithms: If you need a completely new approach to a problem, AI may not be the best source.

Deep Optimization: AI-generated code works but rarely represents the most efficient possible solution.

Project-Specific Knowledge: Without extensive context, AI can't understand the unique aspects of your project.

Guaranteed Correctness: AI suggestions may contain bugs or misunderstandings that require human review.

Long-Term Planning: AI focuses on immediate code generation rather than architectural decisions.

As a beginner, start with smaller, well-defined tasks where AI can provide the most value. As you gain experience, you'll develop a better sense of when to rely on AI suggestions and when to write code manually.

Remember that vibe coding isn't about replacing your skills—it's about amplifying them. The goal isn't to hand all coding tasks to AI but to create a collaborative process where you and the AI each contribute your strengths.

In the next chapter, we'll explore core techniques for vibe coders, including using AI as a first drafter, automating repetitive tasks, and accelerating prototyping. These practical approaches will help you get the most from AI coding assistants in your daily work.

Chapter 3: Core Techniques for Vibe Coders

Mastering vibe coding involves more than just asking AI to write code. The most effective practitioners develop specific techniques that maximize the benefits of AI assistance while maintaining control over the development process. This chapter explores core approaches that will help you become more productive with AI coding tools.

Using AI as a First Drafter

One of the most powerful techniques in vibe coding is treating the AI as your first drafter—the initial creator of code that you'll later review and refine. This approach leverages the AI's speed while preserving your judgment and expertise.

Start with a Clear Specification

Before asking the AI to generate code, take time to clarify what you need:

- What problem does this code solve?
- What inputs will it receive?
- What outputs should it produce?
- What constraints or requirements must it meet?

The more specific your specification, the better the AI's first draft will be. For example:

"Create a Python function that validates email addresses. It should check for proper format (username@domain.tld), verify the domain has at least one period, and ensure the username contains only letters, numbers, periods, underscores, or hyphens. Return True if valid, False otherwise."

This detailed specification gives the AI clear guidance about what you expect.

Request Multiple Approaches

For important functions, ask the AI to provide several implementation options:

"Please show me three different ways to implement this email validation function. One using regular expressions, one using string manipulation methods, and one using Python's built-in email validation libraries if available."

Comparing different approaches helps you understand trade-offs and choose the best solution for your needs.

Review Critically

When you receive the AI's draft, review it with a critical eye:

- Does it meet all requirements from your specification?
- Are there edge cases it might not handle?
- Could it be more efficient or readable?
- Does it follow best practices for your language or framework?

This review process helps you catch issues before they become problems in your codebase.

Refine Iteratively

Use the AI to help refine the initial draft:

"The regex solution looks good, but it doesn't check for the maximum length of an email address. Can you update it to ensure the entire email is no longer than 254 characters, as per RFC 5321?"

Through this back-and-forth process, you guide the AI toward a final solution that meets your exact needs.

Automating Repetitive Tasks

Programming often involves repetitive tasks that follow predictable patterns. AI coding assistants excel at automating these tasks, freeing you to focus on more creative aspects of development.

Code Transformations

AI tools can help with systematic code changes:

- Converting between formats (JSON to XML, CSV to JSON)
- Translating between programming languages
- Updating API calls to match a new version
- Refactoring code to use newer language features

For example:

"I have a collection of JavaScript functions that use callbacks. Please convert them to use Promises instead. Here's an example of one function:

```
function fetchData(url, callback) {
  const xhr = new XMLHttpRequest();
  xhr.open('GET', url);
  xhr.onload = () => {
    if (xhr.status === 200) {
      callback(null, JSON.parse(xhr.responseText));
```

```
  } else {
    callback(new Error(`Request failed with status
${xhr.status}`));
    }
  };
  xhr.onerror = () => callback(new Error('Network
error'));
  xhr.send();
}
```

"

Generating Repetitive Structures

AI can create sets of similar components based on
patterns:

- CRUD operations for database entities
- API endpoints for a REST service
- Form validation rules
- Test cases for a function

For instance:

"Generate mongoose schemas and CRUD operations
for a blog application with the following entities:

1. User (fields: username, email, password, bio, joinDate)
2. Post (fields: title, content, author, tags, publishDate, lastModified)
3. Comment (fields: content, author, post, createdAt)

Include proper validation and relationships between entities."

Documentation Generation

AI can help create and maintain documentation:

- Function and class documentation
- API endpoint descriptions
- README files
- User guides

For example:

"Based on this code, generate JSDoc comments for each function:

```
function calculateTax(amount, rate) {
  return amount * rate / 100;
}
```

```
function formatCurrency(amount, currency = 'USD')
{
  return new Intl.NumberFormat('en-US', {
    style: 'currency',
    currency
  }).format(amount);
}
```

"

By identifying repetitive tasks in your workflow and delegating them to AI, you can significantly increase your productivity while reducing the tedium of routine coding.

Accelerating Prototyping

Prototyping—creating quick, functional versions of software to test ideas—benefits tremendously from AI assistance. Vibe coding allows you to move from concept to working prototype faster than ever before.

Rapid MVP Creation

AI tools excel at generating minimum viable products (MVPs):

"Create a simple React todo list application with the following features:

- Add new tasks
- Mark tasks as complete
- Delete tasks
- Store tasks in local storage so they persist between page reloads

Include basic CSS styling to make it presentable."

From this prompt, you might receive a complete, functional application that you can immediately test and refine.

Exploring Alternative Designs

AI can help you quickly explore different approaches to a problem:

"Show me three different ways to structure a weather application:

1. A single-page application using React
2. A server-rendered application using Node.js and EJS templates
3. A progressive web app with offline capabilities

For each approach, provide the basic file structure and key code components."

This exploration helps you make informed decisions about architecture before investing significant development time.

Visualizing Data and Interfaces

AI can generate visualization code to help you see how your data might look:

"Create a D3.js visualization that shows monthly sales data as a bar chart with the following features:

- Animated transitions when data changes
- Hover tooltips showing exact values
- A legend for different product categories
- Responsive design that works on different screen sizes"

These visualizations help stakeholders understand your concept and provide feedback early in the development process.

Iterative Refinement

As feedback comes in, AI helps you quickly update your prototype:

"The todo list app works well, but users want these additional features:

- Due dates for tasks
- Priority levels (high, medium, low)
- Filtering by completion status and priority
- Sorting by due date

Please update the code to include these features."

This rapid iteration cycle accelerates the feedback loop, helping you converge on a successful design more quickly.

Building Modular Components with AI Suggestions

Complex applications consist of many interconnected components. AI coding assistants can help you build these components in a modular, maintainable way.

Component-Based Requests

Frame your requests around specific, self-contained components:

"Create a reusable pagination component for a React application. It should:

- Accept total items, items per page, and current page as props
- Display page numbers with previous/next buttons
- Allow customization of active page styling
- Include proper accessibility attributes
- Emit events when page changes"

This focused approach results in components that are easier to integrate into your larger application.

Interface-First Design

Ask the AI to define clear interfaces before implementing functionality:

"Design a TypeScript interface for a user authentication service with methods for:

- User registration
- Login/logout
- Password reset
- Session management
- Profile updates

Include proper types for all parameters and return values."

Well-defined interfaces make it easier to connect components and maintain separation of concerns.

Integration Guidance

Request advice on how components should work together:

"I have a user authentication component and a user profile component. Show me how to integrate them so that:

1. The profile component displays user data after successful authentication
2. Profile updates are secured by the authentication system
3. Logging out properly clears profile data"

This guidance helps you maintain clean architecture as your application grows.

Testing Strategies

Ask for testing approaches specific to your components:

"Provide unit tests for the pagination component using Jest and React Testing Library. Include tests for:

- Rendering with different numbers of pages
- Page navigation functionality
- Edge cases like having only one page
- Accessibility compliance"

Component-specific tests help ensure reliability as you assemble your application.

Debugging the AI Way: Iterative Refinement Through Prompts

When code doesn't work as expected, AI tools can help with debugging through an iterative process of analysis and refinement.

Error Analysis

Share error messages with the AI for interpretation:

"I'm getting this error when running my React component:

Error: Objects are not valid as a React child. If you meant to render a collection of children, use an array instead.

Here's my component code:

[paste your code]

What's causing this error and how can I fix it?"

The AI can often identify common mistakes and suggest corrections.

Code Review Requests

Ask the AI to review your code for potential issues:

"Please review this function for bugs, edge cases, or performance issues:

```
function findDuplicates(array) {
  const duplicates = [];
  for (let i = 0; i < array.length; i++) {
    for (let j = i + 1; j < array.length; j++) {
      if (array[i] === array[j] &&
!duplicates.includes(array[i])) {
        duplicates.push(array[i]);
      }
    }
  }
  return duplicates;
}
```

"

This review might catch issues you've overlooked.

Step-by-Step Execution

Ask the AI to trace through code execution:

"Walk through how this function executes with the input [1, 2, 3, 2, 1], showing the values of variables at each step:

```
def find_first_duplicate(nums):
    seen = set()
    for num in nums:
        if num in seen:
            return num
        seen.add(num)
    return -1
```

"

This trace can help you understand where things go wrong.

Alternative Implementations

When debugging proves difficult, ask for a fresh approach:

"I'm struggling to debug this sorting algorithm. Can you provide an alternative implementation that achieves the same result but uses a different approach?"

Sometimes starting fresh is more efficient than fixing a problematic implementation.

Integrating Human Oversight into AI-Driven Workflows

While AI coding assistants offer powerful capabilities, human oversight remains essential. Effective vibe coding integrates human judgment throughout the development process.

Establish Review Checkpoints

Define stages where you'll carefully review AI-generated code:

- After initial generation
- After making significant changes
- Before integration with other components
- Before committing to version control

These checkpoints ensure that no problematic code makes it into your project.

Maintain Coding Standards

Ask the AI to follow your project's standards:

"Please format this code according to our team's style guide:

- Use 2-space indentation
- Place opening braces on the same line
- Use camelCase for variables and functions
- Add JSDoc comments for public functions"

Then verify that the output actually meets these standards.

Understand Before Integrating

Make sure you understand AI-generated code before using it:

"Please explain how this authentication middleware works, particularly the JWT verification part and how it handles expired tokens."

If you can't explain how the code works, you might struggle to maintain it later.

Test Thoroughly

Never assume AI-generated code is correct without testing:

- Write unit tests for core functionality
- Test edge cases explicitly
- Verify performance with realistic data volumes
- Check security implications, especially for code handling sensitive operations

Testing helps catch issues that might not be apparent from code review alone.

Document AI Contributions

Keep track of which parts of your codebase were AI-generated:

- Add comments indicating AI-generated sections
- Document any modifications you made to the generated code
- Note any limitations or assumptions in the implementation

This documentation helps future developers (including your future self) understand the code's origins and evolution.

By applying these core techniques, you'll develop a productive workflow that combines AI's speed and breadth with your judgment and expertise. The next chapter will explore how to evolve this workflow as you gain experience with vibe coding.

Chapter 4: Evolving Your Vibe Coding Workflow

As you gain experience with AI-assisted programming, your approach will naturally evolve. What begins as simple code generation requests gradually transforms into a sophisticated collaboration between you and AI tools. This chapter explores how to advance your vibe coding workflow, moving from basic usage to mastery.

Transforming from a Passive User to an Active Collaborator

Many developers begin their vibe coding journey as passive users—submitting requests and accepting whatever the AI produces. While this approach works for simple tasks, true productivity comes from developing an active collaboration with AI tools.

Recognize the Partnership Dynamic

Think of AI coding assistants as junior developers with unusual characteristics:

- They have broad knowledge but limited depth
- They respond well to clear guidance
- They don't take initiative without direction

- They learn your preferences through interaction

This mental model helps you engage more effectively with AI tools. Rather than simply asking for code, you're guiding a capable but limited partner.

Develop a Feedback Loop

Active collaboration requires consistent feedback:

1. You provide a request with clear specifications
2. The AI generates initial code
3. You review and provide specific feedback
4. The AI refines based on your guidance
5. Repeat until satisfied

This iterative process produces better results than one-off requests. For example:

Initial request: "Create a function to validate form input."

AI response: *[Generates basic validation function]*

Your feedback: "This looks good for text fields, but I also need validation for email addresses, phone numbers, and dates. Can you expand the function to handle these input types?"

AI refinement: *[Updates function with additional validation types]*

Your feedback: "The phone validation needs to accept international formats. Also, can we make this more modular so I can use individual validation types separately?"

Through this conversation, you guide the AI toward a solution that meets your specific needs.

Learn to Read AI-Generated Code

Develop the habit of carefully reading and understanding code before accepting it. Look for:

- Logic errors or edge cases
- Performance implications
- Security considerations
- Maintainability issues

This critical reading skill helps you catch problems early and deepens your understanding of programming patterns.

Take Ownership of the Process

As an active collaborator, you maintain control over:

- The problem definition
- Architectural decisions
- Quality standards
- Final implementation choices

The AI serves your vision, not the other way around. This ownership mindset ensures that your projects reflect your intentions and standards.

Guiding AI to Meet Specific Goals

As your collaboration skills develop, you'll learn to guide AI tools toward specific outcomes through targeted prompting techniques.

Set Clear Constraints

Explicitly state limitations and requirements:

"Generate a sorting function that:

- Uses no more than $O(n \log n)$ time complexity
- Works with arrays of any size
- Handles duplicate values correctly
- Uses only built-in JavaScript methods
- Includes detailed comments explaining the algorithm"

These constraints focus the AI on solutions that meet your exact needs.

Provide Context About Users and Environment

Help the AI understand who will use the code and under what conditions:

"This code will be used by junior developers maintaining a legacy system with Internet Explorer 11 compatibility requirements. Avoid modern JavaScript features like arrow functions, template literals, or optional chaining."

This context helps the AI generate appropriate solutions for your specific situation.

Request Specific Patterns or Approaches

Guide the AI toward your preferred coding style:

"Please implement this using the repository pattern with dependency injection. Follow SOLID principles and separate the business logic from data access concerns."

This direction helps align the generated code with your architectural vision.

Ask for Explanations of Trade-offs

Request that the AI explain its choices:

"When generating this caching solution, please explain the trade-offs between memory usage and performance for each approach you consider."

These explanations help you make informed decisions about the final implementation.

Use Reference Examples

Show the AI examples of code that matches your desired style or approach:

"Here's an example of how we structure components in our application:

// Example component

Please follow this pattern when creating the new user profile component."

Reference examples provide concrete guidance that helps the AI match your expectations.

Fine-tuning Generated Code for Better Optimization

AI-generated code typically prioritizes correctness over optimization. As you evolve your workflow, you'll learn to fine-tune this code for better performance, readability, and maintainability.

Identify Optimization Opportunities

Review generated code with an eye for improvement:

- Redundant operations
- Inefficient data structures
- Unnecessary memory usage
- Overly complex algorithms

For example, you might notice that an AI-generated function creates multiple copies of a large array when a single pass would suffice.

Request Specific Optimizations

Ask the AI to improve particular aspects of the code:

"This database query function works correctly, but it might be inefficient for large datasets. Can you optimize it to:

1. Reduce the number of database calls
2. Use query parameters to prevent SQL injection
3. Add appropriate indexing suggestions

4. Implement connection pooling"

These targeted requests help the AI focus on the most important optimizations.

Balance Readability and Performance

Sometimes the most efficient code is hard to understand. Ask for a balance:

"Please optimize this function for processing large files, but maintain readability. Add comments explaining any complex optimizations so other developers can understand the approach."

This balance ensures that optimized code remains maintainable.

Test Before and After

Measure the impact of optimizations:

"I've implemented your suggested optimizations. The function now runs 40% faster but uses slightly more memory. Can you suggest ways to reduce the memory footprint while preserving the performance gain?"

This data-driven approach helps you make informed decisions about optimization trade-offs.

Learn from AI Optimizations

Pay attention to the optimization techniques the AI suggests. You might discover:

- Language features you weren't using
- Library functions that simplify your code
- Algorithm improvements
- Design patterns that enhance performance

These insights build your optimization skills for future projects.

Managing Mid-Complexity Projects with AI

As you become more comfortable with vibe coding, you'll tackle increasingly complex projects. Mid-complexity projects—those too large for a single prompt but not requiring enterprise architecture—present unique challenges and opportunities.

Break Down Projects into Components

Divide your project into manageable pieces:

- Core data models
- Business logic modules

- User interface components
- External integrations

Then address each component with focused AI prompts.

Maintain a Project Specification

Create a central document describing:

- Project goals and requirements
- Component interactions
- Data structures
- API contracts
- Coding standards

Reference this specification in your prompts to maintain consistency across components.

Develop Incrementally

Build your project in small, testable increments:

1. Create core data structures
2. Implement basic functionality
3. Add features one by one
4. Refine and optimize

This approach allows you to verify each piece before moving on, reducing the risk of major issues later.

Create Integration Points

Pay special attention to how components connect:

"I have a user authentication service and a content management system. Please create an integration layer that:

1. Passes user credentials from the auth service to the CMS
2. Enforces content access permissions based on user roles
3. Logs access attempts for security auditing"

Well-defined integration points help components work together smoothly.

Maintain a Testing Strategy

As projects grow, testing becomes more important:

"Generate unit tests for this payment processing module. Include tests for:

- Successful transactions
- Failed transactions due to insufficient funds

- Network errors during processing
- Invalid payment information
- Proper handling of duplicate payment attempts"

Comprehensive testing helps catch issues that might not be apparent in isolated components.

Keeping the Focus on Maintainability and Scalability

As your projects grow, maintainability and scalability become increasingly important. Evolving your vibe coding workflow means thinking beyond immediate functionality to long-term code health.

Request Modular Designs

Ask for code structured for future expansion:

"Please design this notification system to be modular, so we can easily add new notification channels (beyond the current email and SMS) without modifying existing code."

This forward-thinking approach saves time when requirements change.

Emphasize Documentation

Make documentation a priority in your requests:

"Along with the code, please provide:

- A README explaining the purpose and usage
- Function-level documentation
- A simple example demonstrating basic usage
- Notes about any assumptions or limitations"

Good documentation makes your code more maintainable by future developers (including yourself).

Consider Performance at Scale

Ask the AI to consider how code will perform as usage grows:

"This user management system needs to handle up to 100,000 active users. Please implement the search functionality with this scale in mind, including appropriate caching and database query optimization."

This scalability focus helps avoid painful rewrites as your application grows.

Plan for Configuration and Customization

Request designs that separate configuration from code:

"Design this logging system to be configurable through external settings, allowing users to change log levels, output formats, and destinations without code modifications."

This separation makes your code more adaptable to different environments and requirements.

Ask About Maintenance Concerns

Prompt the AI to identify potential maintenance issues:

"What parts of this code might be difficult to maintain in the future? Are there any dependencies or approaches that could cause problems as the project evolves?"

This foresight helps you address maintenance concerns before they become problems.

As you evolve your vibe coding workflow, you'll develop a more sophisticated relationship with AI tools. You'll move from simply generating code to collaboratively creating software that's not just functional but also optimized, maintainable, and scalable. This evolution multiplies the benefits of AI assistance while maintaining your control over the development process.

In the next chapter, we'll explore advanced techniques that push the boundaries of what's possible with AI-assisted programming.

Chapter 5: Advanced Techniques in Vibe Coding

As you become more comfortable with AI-assisted programming, you can explore advanced techniques that push the boundaries of what's possible. These approaches go beyond basic code generation to create sophisticated workflows that maximize both human creativity and AI capabilities.

Multi-agent Systems: Using Multiple AI Tools in Tandem

While a single AI coding assistant offers significant benefits, combining multiple specialized tools can create a powerful development ecosystem. This multi-agent approach allows you to leverage the unique strengths of different AI systems.

Specialized Tools for Specialized Tasks

Different AI tools excel at different aspects of development:

- Some provide excellent code completion within your editor
- Others offer strong conversational interfaces for discussing complex problems

- Some specialize in specific languages or frameworks
- Others focus on particular tasks like refactoring or optimization

By identifying the strengths of each tool, you can direct tasks to the most appropriate assistant.

Creating Workflows Across Tools

Develop processes that move work between different AI assistants:

1. Use a conversational AI to explore high-level design options
2. Take the chosen design to a code-focused AI for implementation
3. Use a specialized AI for testing and quality assurance
4. Return to the conversational AI to explain the implementation and document it

This workflow leverages each tool's strengths while minimizing its weaknesses.

Handling Contradictions and Conflicts

When using multiple AI tools, you may receive conflicting advice or incompatible code. Develop strategies for resolving these conflicts:

- Evaluate each suggestion based on your knowledge and project requirements
- Ask each AI to critique the other's approach (without revealing it came from another AI)
- Test competing implementations to compare performance or maintainability
- Create hybrid solutions that combine the best aspects of different suggestions

As the human in the loop, you make the final decisions when AI tools disagree.

Maintaining Consistency Across Tools

To ensure coherent results when using multiple AI assistants:

- Create a project style guide that you share with each tool
- Use consistent terminology and naming conventions in all prompts
- Maintain a central repository of code snippets and design decisions

- Periodically review the overall architecture to ensure alignment

This consistency helps create a unified codebase despite using diverse AI tools.

Leveraging AI to Design and Structure Architectures

While AI coding assistants excel at generating individual components, they can also help with higher-level architectural decisions when properly guided.

Exploring Architectural Patterns

Ask AI tools to suggest appropriate architectural patterns for your project:

"I'm building a real-time collaborative document editor. What architectural patterns would be appropriate for this application? For each suggested pattern, please explain:

- How it addresses the real-time collaboration requirement
- Its scalability characteristics
- Potential implementation challenges

- When this pattern might be preferred over alternatives"

This exploration helps you understand options before committing to an approach.

Visualizing System Components

Request visual representations of proposed architectures:

"Based on our discussion of a microservices architecture for the e-commerce platform, please describe how you would structure the system components. Include:

- Key services and their responsibilities
- Communication patterns between services
- Data storage considerations
- External integration points"

While most AI tools can't directly create diagrams, their textual descriptions can help you visualize the architecture.

Evaluating Trade-offs

Ask the AI to analyze trade-offs between different architectural choices:

"I'm considering both GraphQL and REST for our API. Please compare these approaches for our specific use case, considering:

- Client flexibility and development experience
- Server implementation complexity
- Performance characteristics with our expected data patterns
- Long-term maintenance considerations"

This analysis helps you make informed architectural decisions.

Incremental Architecture Development

Use AI to help evolve your architecture incrementally:

1. Start with a minimal viable architecture
2. Implement core functionality
3. Identify pain points or limitations
4. Ask the AI for targeted improvements
5. Implement changes and evaluate results
6. Repeat as needed

This approach allows your architecture to grow organically based on actual needs rather than speculative planning.

Push the AI Boundaries: Experimentation with Unconventional Workflows

The most advanced vibe coders don't just follow established patterns—they experiment with new approaches that push the boundaries of what's possible with AI assistance.

Pair Programming with AI

Develop a pair programming dynamic with your AI assistant:

1. You write some code
2. The AI suggests improvements or next steps
3. You accept, modify, or reject the suggestions
4. The AI explains its reasoning
5. You continue the development together

This collaborative approach combines human creativity with AI suggestions in real-time.

Competitive Programming

Challenge the AI to solve the same problem you're working on:

1. Define a programming challenge
2. Implement your own solution

3. Ask the AI to solve the same problem
4. Compare approaches and performance
5. Learn from any differences

This friendly competition can reveal alternative approaches and help you improve your skills.

Reverse Engineering

Use AI to help understand complex code:

1. Provide a code snippet you don't fully understand
2. Ask the AI to explain how it works
3. Request simpler versions that maintain the same functionality
4. Gradually build your understanding of the complex implementation

This technique helps you learn from existing code and improve your comprehension skills.

Prompt Engineering Experiments

Systematically test different prompting approaches:

1. Create a specific coding task
2. Try various prompting styles (direct requests, examples, constraints, etc.)

3. Compare the results
4. Document which approaches work best for different types of tasks

These experiments help you develop more effective communication with AI tools.

Balancing Speed and Accuracy in AI-Driven Outputs

One of the most challenging aspects of advanced vibe coding is finding the right balance between development speed and code quality. AI tools can generate code quickly, but that speed sometimes comes at the cost of accuracy or optimization.

Tiered Quality Requirements

Establish different quality tiers for different parts of your codebase:

- Critical components: Highest scrutiny, extensive testing, manual review
- Core functionality: Careful review, good test coverage
- Utility functions: Basic review, standard tests
- Experimental features: Rapid iteration, minimal verification

This tiered approach helps you allocate your attention where it matters most.

Progressive Refinement

Adopt a workflow that progressively improves code quality:

1. Generate a quick, functional implementation
2. Test the basic functionality
3. Identify areas for improvement
4. Request targeted optimizations
5. Add comprehensive error handling
6. Enhance documentation
7. Finalize with thorough testing

This approach gives you working code quickly while still reaching high quality in the final version.

Automated Quality Checks

Integrate automated tools to verify AI-generated code:

- Linters to check for style and potential issues
- Static analysis tools to identify bugs or vulnerabilities

- Performance benchmarks to catch inefficient implementations
- Type checkers to verify correct usage

These automated checks provide a safety net that helps you move quickly without sacrificing quality.

Contextual Speed/Quality Decisions

Make deliberate decisions about when to prioritize speed versus quality:

- Early prototyping: Favor speed to quickly test ideas
- Core algorithms: Favor quality to ensure correctness and performance
- User-facing features: Balance speed and quality based on impact
- Infrastructure code: Favor quality for stability and security

These contextual decisions help you optimize your development process for different situations.

Learning from Mistakes

When AI-generated code contains errors, use these as learning opportunities:

1. Analyze what went wrong
2. Identify how your prompt might have contributed to the error
3. Develop strategies to prevent similar issues
4. Document the lesson for future reference

This continuous improvement process helps you balance speed and accuracy more effectively over time.

Advanced vibe coding techniques require practice and experimentation. As you push the boundaries of what's possible with AI assistance, you'll develop unique workflows that match your personal style and project needs. The most successful vibe coders maintain a spirit of curiosity, constantly exploring new approaches while building on proven techniques.

In the next chapter, we'll examine the challenges that come with AI-assisted programming and strategies for overcoming them.

Chapter 6: Challenges in Vibe Coding

While AI-assisted programming offers tremendous benefits, it also presents unique challenges. Understanding these challenges and developing strategies to address them will help you avoid common pitfalls and use vibe coding more effectively.

Common Pitfalls in AI-Assisted Programming

Even experienced developers can fall into traps when working with AI coding assistants. Recognizing these common pitfalls is the first step toward avoiding them.

Accepting Code Without Understanding

One of the most dangerous pitfalls is implementing AI-generated code without fully understanding how it works. This can lead to:

- Difficulty debugging when problems arise
- Challenges when extending or modifying the code later
- Security vulnerabilities you're unaware of
- Performance issues that aren't immediately obvious

Always take time to understand code before integrating it into your project. If something isn't clear, ask the AI to explain it or break it down into simpler components.

Prompt Tunnel Vision

When a prompt doesn't produce the expected results, many developers fall into a pattern of making minor adjustments to the same basic request. This "prompt tunnel vision" can waste time when a completely different approach might work better.

If you're not getting good results after 2-3 refinements, try:

- Restructuring your request completely
- Breaking the problem into smaller parts
- Providing different examples or context
- Switching to a different AI tool

Misaligned Expectations

Setting unrealistic expectations for what AI can do leads to frustration. Remember that AI coding assistants:

- Don't truly understand your business domain

- Can't read your mind about unstated requirements
- May not know about very recent technologies or libraries
- Don't have access to your private codebases unless you share them

Align your expectations with these limitations to avoid disappointment.

Overcomplicating Simple Tasks

Sometimes using AI adds unnecessary complexity to simple tasks. If you can write a straightforward function in two minutes, taking five minutes to craft the perfect prompt might not be efficient.

Develop a sense for when AI assistance adds value and when traditional coding is more practical.

Neglecting to Verify Generated Code

AI-generated code often works for the happy path but fails in edge cases. Common verification gaps include:

- Not testing with boundary values
- Failing to check error handling

- Overlooking performance with large inputs
- Not verifying security practices

Always verify AI-generated code as thoroughly as you would verify code written by a junior developer.

Over-reliance on Generated Code

As you become comfortable with AI assistance, the temptation to rely too heavily on generated code can grow. This over-reliance brings several risks.

Skill Atrophy

If you always ask AI to write code for you, your own coding skills may deteriorate. This creates a dangerous dependency:

- You become less able to evaluate the quality of AI suggestions
- Your ability to solve novel problems diminishes
- You struggle when working in environments where AI tools aren't available

To prevent skill atrophy:

- Regularly write code without AI assistance

- Challenge yourself to understand and modify AI-generated code
- Use AI as a learning tool by asking it to explain its approaches

Loss of Creative Problem-Solving

AI coding assistants excel at implementing known patterns but rarely produce truly innovative solutions. Over-reliance can lead to:

- Conventional approaches to problems that might benefit from fresh thinking
- Missed opportunities for creative optimizations
- Homogenized code that looks like everyone else's solutions

Balance AI assistance with your own creative thinking to avoid this trap.

Reduced Ownership and Pride

Writing code yourself creates a sense of ownership and pride that can be diminished when relying heavily on AI. This psychological aspect affects:

- Your motivation and satisfaction

- Your willingness to maintain and improve the code
- Your confidence as a developer

Find a balance that preserves your sense of ownership while leveraging AI benefits.

Dependency on External Services

Many AI coding tools are cloud-based services that could:

- Change their pricing or terms
- Alter their capabilities
- Experience outages
- Shut down entirely

Maintain the ability to work effectively without these tools to reduce your vulnerability to such changes.

Debugging Errors Without Understanding the Underlying Logic

When AI generates complex code, debugging becomes challenging if you don't understand the underlying logic. This challenge requires specific strategies.

Systematic Decomposition

Break complex functions into smaller parts:

1. Identify the main components of the AI-generated code
2. Extract each component into a separate function
3. Test each function independently
4. Recombine once you understand each part

This divide-and-conquer approach makes complex code more manageable.

Instrumentation and Logging

Add extensive logging to track the code's behavior:

- Log input values at function entry points
- Track state changes throughout execution
- Record decision points and branch selections
- Capture output values before they're returned

These breadcrumbs help you follow the execution path and identify where things go wrong.

Comparative Debugging

Create a simpler version of the functionality:

1. Implement a basic version that you fully understand
2. Compare its behavior with the AI-generated version
3. Identify differences in output or behavior
4. Use these differences to locate issues in the complex version

This comparison provides insights into how the AI-generated code works.

Leveraging AI for Explanation

Use AI to help understand the code it generated:

- Ask for line-by-line explanations
- Request simplified versions that maintain core functionality
- Have it identify potential failure points
- Ask about the reasoning behind specific implementation choices

This approach uses AI as a teaching tool rather than just a code generator.

Security Concerns in AI-Generated Applications

AI coding assistants may generate code with security vulnerabilities if not properly guided. This risk requires special attention.

Common Vulnerability Types

Be particularly vigilant about these common issues in AI-generated code:

- **Injection Vulnerabilities**: Improper handling of user input that could allow SQL injection, cross-site scripting, or command injection
- **Authentication Weaknesses**: Insufficient protection of login systems, session management, or credential handling
- **Authorization Flaws**: Inadequate checking of user permissions or access rights
- **Data Exposure**: Unintended revelation of sensitive information through logs, error messages, or APIs
- **Dependency Issues**: Use of outdated or vulnerable libraries

Explicitly ask the AI to address these concerns in security-sensitive code.

Security-Focused Prompting

Include security requirements in your prompts:

"Create a user registration function that:

- Securely hashes passwords using bcrypt
- Validates and sanitizes all user inputs
- Prevents username enumeration attacks
- Implements rate limiting for failed attempts
- Logs security events without exposing sensitive data"

These explicit requirements help the AI generate more secure code.

Security Review Process

Establish a dedicated security review for AI-generated code:

1. Identify security-sensitive components
2. Apply extra scrutiny to authentication, authorization, and data handling
3. Use security scanning tools to check for known vulnerabilities
4. Conduct manual reviews focusing on business logic flaws
5. Test with security-focused scenarios

This process helps catch issues before they reach production.

Learning from Security Incidents

When security issues are found:

1. Analyze the root cause
2. Identify how your prompting or review process missed it
3. Update your security guidelines
4. Create example prompts that address similar vulnerabilities
5. Share lessons learned with your team

This continuous improvement helps prevent similar issues in the future.

Managing Technical Debt Arising from Poorly Validated AI Outputs

AI-generated code can create technical debt—future costs resulting from quick solutions now—if not properly validated and refined.

Identifying AI-Specific Technical Debt

Look for these warning signs in AI-generated code:

- **Unnecessary Complexity**: Overly elaborate solutions to simple problems
- **Inconsistent Patterns**: Different approaches to similar problems throughout the codebase
- **Redundant Code**: Duplicated functionality that could be consolidated
- **Outdated Practices**: Use of deprecated methods or libraries
- **Poor Naming**: Generic or confusing variable and function names
- **Missing Documentation**: Code that works but lacks explanatory comments

These issues compound over time if not addressed.

Technical Debt Budgeting

Allocate time specifically for managing technical debt:

- Schedule regular refactoring sessions
- Address debt immediately for critical components
- Maintain a backlog of technical debt items
- Balance new feature development with debt reduction

This budgeting prevents technical debt from accumulating to unmanageable levels.

Refactoring Strategies

Develop approaches for efficiently refactoring AI-generated code:

1. Start with high-impact, low-effort improvements
2. Create consistent patterns and apply them throughout the codebase
3. Extract reusable components from duplicated code
4. Improve naming and documentation to clarify intent
5. Update to current best practices and libraries

These strategies help you systematically reduce technical debt.

Preventive Measures

Implement practices that prevent technical debt from forming:

- Create templates for common components

- Establish coding standards specific to AI-generated code
- Develop a library of well-validated, reusable functions
- Implement automated quality checks
- Conduct regular code reviews focused on consistency and maintainability

These preventive measures reduce the need for later refactoring.

Handling Edge Cases and Unexpected AI Behavior

AI coding assistants sometimes produce unexpected results or fail to handle edge cases properly. Managing these situations requires specific techniques.

Systematic Edge Case Identification

Develop a process for identifying potential edge cases:

- Empty or null inputs
- Boundary values (minimum, maximum, zero)
- Malformed data
- Unexpected data types

- Resource limitations (memory, time, connections)
- Concurrent access scenarios

Explicitly test these cases with AI-generated code.

Graceful Degradation Planning

Design systems to handle AI failures gracefully:

- Implement fallback mechanisms
- Add timeout handling
- Create circuit breakers for external dependencies
- Design user experiences that accommodate partial functionality
- Log failures for later analysis and improvement

These measures maintain system stability even when components don't work as expected.

Feedback Collection and Analysis

Gather information about unexpected AI behavior:

- Log unusual outputs or recommendations
- Track patterns in AI failures

- Analyze which types of requests produce inconsistent results
- Identify common characteristics of problematic prompts

This analysis helps you avoid conditions that lead to unreliable results.

Continuous Learning Loop

Establish a process for improving your AI interactions based on experience:

1. Document unexpected behaviors
2. Analyze root causes
3. Develop improved prompting techniques
4. Create test cases that verify fixes
5. Share knowledge with your team

This learning loop gradually reduces the frequency and impact of unexpected AI behavior.

By acknowledging these challenges and developing strategies to address them, you can use vibe coding more effectively while avoiding its potential pitfalls. The most successful AI-assisted developers maintain a balanced approach—leveraging AI capabilities while applying human judgment, creativity, and critical thinking.

In the next chapter, we'll explore the human element in vibe coding and how experienced developers can enhance AI workflows.

Chapter 7: The Human Element in Vibe Coding

While AI tools have transformed programming, the human element remains crucial. Experienced developers bring unique value to AI-assisted workflows through their judgment, creativity, and domain knowledge. This chapter explores how human expertise enhances vibe coding and why the partnership between developers and AI produces better results than either could achieve alone.

How Experienced Developers Can Enhance AI Workflows

Experienced developers bring several key strengths to AI-assisted programming that complement and enhance what AI tools can do.

Pattern Recognition Across Projects

Seasoned developers recognize patterns across different projects and domains. This broader perspective allows them to:

- Identify when an AI-suggested solution might work well in the current context

- Spot potential issues based on past experiences with similar code
- Apply lessons learned from previous projects to current challenges
- Recognize when a standard pattern needs customization for specific requirements

This cross-project pattern recognition helps guide AI tools toward appropriate solutions.

Architectural Vision

Experienced developers maintain a clear vision of the overall system architecture. This vision helps them:

- Place AI-generated components within the larger system context
- Ensure consistent design patterns across the codebase
- Guide AI tools to create code that aligns with architectural goals
- Identify when generated code might create architectural problems

By maintaining this big-picture view, developers ensure that AI contributions strengthen rather than undermine the system architecture.

Quality Standards Enforcement

Developers with strong quality standards bring critical evaluation skills:

- They recognize code smells and anti-patterns in AI-generated code
- They apply consistent standards across both human-written and AI-generated components
- They know when to reject or refine AI suggestions that don't meet quality thresholds
- They balance pragmatism with perfectionism based on project needs

These quality standards prevent the accumulation of problematic code, regardless of its source.

Domain Knowledge Application

Perhaps most importantly, experienced developers bring domain knowledge that AI tools lack:

- Understanding of the business context and user needs
- Awareness of industry-specific requirements and regulations
- Knowledge of domain-specific edge cases and constraints

- Familiarity with specialized terminology and concepts

This domain knowledge helps developers guide AI tools to create solutions that address the actual problem, not just the technical aspects.

Acting as Editors and Architects for AI

One of the most valuable roles experienced developers play in vibe coding is that of editor and architect—shaping and refining AI contributions rather than simply accepting them.

Editorial Review Process

Develop a systematic review process for AI-generated code:

1. **Initial Assessment**: Quickly evaluate if the code addresses the core requirements
2. **Structural Review**: Examine the overall organization and approach
3. **Detailed Inspection**: Check specific implementations for correctness and style
4. **Integration Evaluation**: Consider how the code fits with existing components

5. **Refinement Guidance**: Provide specific feedback for improvements

This editorial process improves quality while teaching the AI your preferences over time.

Architectural Guidance

Provide clear architectural direction to AI tools:

- Define component boundaries and responsibilities before requesting implementations
- Establish communication patterns between components
- Specify error handling and logging approaches
- Set performance and scalability expectations

This guidance helps AI tools generate code that fits seamlessly into your architecture.

Style and Convention Enforcement

Maintain consistent style and conventions across your codebase:

- Create style guides that you can reference in prompts

- Review AI-generated code for adherence to these standards
- Request modifications to align with your conventions
- Use automated tools to enforce style consistency

This consistency makes the codebase more maintainable, regardless of whether humans or AI wrote specific parts.

Iterative Refinement

Approach editing as an iterative process:

1. Request an initial implementation
2. Provide specific feedback on what works and what needs improvement
3. Ask for refinements based on your feedback
4. Repeat until the code meets your standards

This collaborative refinement process often produces better results than either human-only or AI-only approaches.

The Importance of Testing and Validating Code

Testing remains essential in the age of AI-assisted programming—perhaps even more so given the potential for subtle issues in generated code.

Comprehensive Test Coverage

Develop tests that verify all aspects of AI-generated code:

- **Functional Testing**: Does the code do what it's supposed to do?
- **Edge Case Testing**: How does it handle boundary conditions and unusual inputs?
- **Performance Testing**: Does it meet efficiency requirements?
- **Integration Testing**: Does it work correctly with other components?
- **Security Testing**: Is it resistant to common vulnerabilities?

This comprehensive testing catches issues that might not be apparent from code review alone.

Test-Driven Approaches

Consider writing tests before requesting code:

1. Define the expected behavior through test cases

2. Share these tests with the AI when requesting an implementation
3. Run the tests against the generated code
4. Refine the implementation until all tests pass

This approach clarifies your expectations and provides an objective measure of success.

Validation Beyond Testing

Extend validation beyond automated tests:

- **Code Reviews**: Have team members review critical AI-generated components
- **Static Analysis**: Use tools to identify potential issues
- **User Acceptance Testing**: Verify that the code meets actual user needs
- **Production Monitoring**: Watch for unexpected behavior in real-world use

This multi-layered validation provides confidence in the reliability of AI-generated code.

Learning from Test Failures

When tests reveal issues in AI-generated code:

1. Analyze the root cause of the failure

2. Identify patterns in the types of issues that occur
3. Update your prompting strategies to prevent similar issues
4. Create test cases that specifically check for these issues in the future

This learning process improves both your testing and your use of AI tools.

Retaining Problem-Solving Skills in an AI-Dominated Workflow

As AI tools handle more coding tasks, deliberately maintaining your problem-solving skills becomes increasingly important.

Regular Skill Practice

Set aside time for coding without AI assistance:

- Solve programming challenges manually
- Implement key algorithms from scratch
- Refactor existing code without AI suggestions
- Debug complex issues using your own analysis

This practice keeps your fundamental skills sharp even as you leverage AI for productivity.

Understanding Before Implementing

Make a habit of understanding problems before asking AI for solutions:

1. Define the problem clearly in your own words
2. Sketch possible approaches
3. Identify potential challenges and edge cases
4. Only then ask AI for implementation help

This approach ensures you're guiding the AI with your understanding rather than delegating your thinking.

Deliberate Learning

Use AI tools as learning opportunities:

- Ask for explanations of generated code
- Request alternative approaches and compare them
- Challenge yourself to predict what the AI will suggest
- Modify AI-generated code to improve it

This deliberate learning turns AI assistance into a growth opportunity rather than a crutch.

Teaching and Mentoring

Explaining concepts to others reinforces your own understanding:

- Mentor junior developers in both traditional and AI-assisted programming
- Document your approaches to vibe coding
- Share insights about effective AI collaboration
- Teach others how to evaluate AI-generated code

Teaching others helps solidify your knowledge and identify gaps in your understanding.

Collaboration Between Developers and AI Tools

The most productive relationship between developers and AI tools is a true collaboration, with each contributing their strengths to create better outcomes than either could achieve alone.

Clear Role Definition

Define clear roles in the collaborative process:

- **AI Tools**: Generate initial code, suggest completions, identify potential issues

- **Human Developer**: Define problems, provide context, evaluate suggestions, make architectural decisions

This role clarity helps you leverage the strengths of both human and AI contributors.

Effective Communication Patterns

Develop communication patterns that enhance collaboration:

- Be explicit about constraints and requirements
- Provide context about why you're making certain requests
- Ask for explanations when you don't understand suggestions
- Provide specific feedback rather than vague criticism

These communication patterns improve the quality of AI responses over time.

Balanced Workload Distribution

Distribute work based on comparative advantages:

- Assign repetitive, well-defined tasks to AI tools

- Reserve creative problem-solving and architectural decisions for humans
- Use AI for initial drafts and humans for refinement
- Let humans handle domain-specific logic while AI handles boilerplate

This balanced distribution maximizes productivity while maintaining quality.

Continuous Improvement Focus

Approach the collaboration as an evolving relationship:

- Track which types of requests yield the best results
- Note patterns in areas where AI suggestions need the most revision
- Refine your prompting techniques based on experience
- Share effective collaboration strategies with your team

This improvement focus helps the human-AI partnership grow stronger over time.

The human element in vibe coding isn't just about filling gaps in AI capabilities—it's about creating a synergy where the combination of human and AI contributions exceeds what either could produce independently. By embracing your role as editor, architect, validator, and collaborator, you can create a productive partnership that leverages the best of both human creativity and AI efficiency.

In the next chapter, we'll explore how this human-AI collaboration can build better software through user-centric development principles and feedback-driven improvement.

Chapter 8: Building Better Software with AI

AI-assisted programming isn't just about writing code faster—it's about creating better software. When used thoughtfully, vibe coding can enhance the quality of your applications by allowing you to focus more on user needs, incorporate feedback more efficiently, and iterate more rapidly. This chapter explores how to leverage AI tools to build software that truly serves its users.

Aligning AI Coding with User-Centric Development Principles

User-centric development puts user needs at the center of the design and development process. AI tools can support this approach when properly guided.

Starting with User Stories

Begin your AI prompts with clear user stories:

"I need a form component for a healthcare application. Users are elderly patients who may have vision impairments and limited technology experience. They need to enter their medication schedule with minimal frustration. The form should be extremely readable, forgiving of errors, and provide clear guidance."

This user-focused context helps the AI generate code that addresses actual human needs rather than just technical requirements.

Accessibility-First Requests

Explicitly include accessibility requirements in your prompts:

"Create a dropdown menu component that:

- Is fully keyboard navigable
- Works with screen readers
- Has sufficient color contrast
- Includes proper ARIA attributes
- Provides visible focus indicators
- Handles touch interfaces for mobile users"

These specific requirements help ensure that AI-generated components work for all users.

Simplicity and Clarity Goals

Ask for solutions that prioritize user understanding:

"Generate a data visualization for financial information. The users are not financial experts, so the visualization should:

- Use simple, intuitive representations
- Avoid jargon and technical terms
- Include clear labels and legends
- Highlight important patterns
- Provide context for interpreting the data"

This guidance helps the AI create outputs that communicate effectively with actual users.

Cross-Platform Considerations

Include diverse user environments in your requirements:

"This authentication flow will be used on devices ranging from old smartphones to desktop computers. The implementation should:

- Be responsive to different screen sizes
- Work with both touch and mouse interactions
- Function on low-bandwidth connections
- Minimize battery usage on mobile devices
- Handle intermittent connectivity gracefully"

These considerations help create software that works well in real-world conditions.

Using Feedback Loops to Refine the AI's Output

One of the greatest strengths of vibe coding is the ability to rapidly incorporate feedback and iterate on solutions. Establishing effective feedback loops maximizes this benefit.

Structured Feedback Process

Develop a systematic approach to providing feedback on AI-generated code:

1. **Functionality Assessment**: Does it work as expected?
2. **User Experience Evaluation**: Is it intuitive and pleasant to use?
3. **Performance Review**: Does it operate efficiently?
4. **Accessibility Check**: Can all users interact with it effectively?
5. **Security Analysis**: Does it protect user data and system integrity?

This structured approach ensures comprehensive feedback that addresses all important aspects.

Incremental Refinement

Use small, focused feedback cycles:

"The search function works well, but users report three issues:

1. Results appear too slowly on mobile devices
2. The sorting options are confusing
3. Recent searches aren't saved between sessions

Let's address these one by one, starting with the performance issue on mobile."

This incremental approach makes improvements more manageable and trackable.

Comparative Feedback

Help the AI understand your preferences through comparisons:

"Between these two implementations of the shopping cart, I prefer the second one because:

- The visual hierarchy makes the total price more prominent
- The quantity controls are more intuitive

- Error messages appear inline rather than as popups
- The checkout button is more accessible

Can you revise the first implementation to incorporate these strengths?"

This comparative feedback helps the AI learn your quality standards.

User Testing Integration

Incorporate actual user feedback into your AI prompts:

"We conducted usability testing on the registration form, and users struggled with these aspects:

1. The password requirements weren't clear until after submission
2. The 'Next' button location was inconsistent between steps
3. Error messages disappeared too quickly to be read

Please update the form to address these specific issues."

This direct connection to user experiences keeps development focused on real needs.

The Role of Behavioral Data in Guiding the Coding Process

Behavioral data—information about how users actually interact with your software—provides valuable insights that can guide your vibe coding process.

Data-Informed Prompts

Include behavioral insights in your requests:

"Our analytics show that 70% of users abandon our checkout process on the payment page. Heatmap data indicates they're confused by the credit card form. Please redesign this component with a focus on clarity and simplicity, especially for first-time users."

These data points help the AI understand the real-world problem it's solving.

A/B Testing Preparation

Use AI to generate variants for testing:

"Create three different versions of our signup flow:

1. A minimalist version with a single form
2. A step-by-step wizard approach
3. A social-first version that prioritizes third-party authentication

We'll A/B test these to see which performs best with our target audience."

This approach leverages AI to explore multiple solutions that can be validated with real users.

Behavioral Pattern Recognition

Share observed user patterns to inform design decisions:

"Our data shows that users typically search for products, then filter by price, then sort by reviews. However, our current interface requires too many clicks for this common path. Please redesign the search results page to streamline this specific workflow."

These behavioral insights help create interfaces that align with actual usage patterns.

Continuous Improvement Cycle

Establish a cycle that incorporates behavioral data:

1. Generate initial implementation with AI
2. Deploy and collect usage data
3. Analyze behavioral patterns and pain points
4. Feed insights back into AI prompts for improvements
5. Repeat with each iteration

This data-driven cycle leads to progressively better user experiences.

Iterative Improvements: Enhancing Software with AI Insights

AI tools can help analyze existing software and suggest improvements based on code patterns, user feedback, and industry best practices.

Code Quality Enhancements

Ask AI to suggest improvements to existing code:

"Review this authentication module for:

- Security vulnerabilities
- Performance bottlenecks
- Maintainability issues
- Potential bugs
- Accessibility concerns

Suggest specific improvements for each issue you identify."

These targeted reviews help systematically enhance your codebase.

Feature Expansion Guidance

Use AI to explore feature enhancements:

"Our users love the basic version of our task management app, but we want to add more value. Based on the current implementation, what are the most natural next features we could add that would enhance the user experience without overcomplicating the interface?"

This guidance helps you evolve your software in ways that align with its current strengths.

Refactoring Assistance

Leverage AI for code restructuring:

"This component has grown organically and become difficult to maintain. Please suggest a refactoring that:

- Breaks it into smaller, more focused components

- Improves state management
- Reduces prop drilling
- Maintains all current functionality
- Preserves the existing API for backward compatibility"

This assistance makes complex refactoring more approachable.

Technical Debt Reduction

Identify and address accumulated technical issues:

"Our codebase has accumulated technical debt in these areas:

- Inconsistent error handling
- Duplicate utility functions
- Mixed styling approaches
- Outdated API usage

Please provide a prioritized plan for addressing these issues, starting with the highest-impact improvements."

This systematic approach helps reduce technical debt without overwhelming your team.

Documentation Improvements

Enhance understanding of your codebase:

"Generate comprehensive documentation for this payment processing module, including:

- High-level architecture overview
- Function-by-function explanations
- Data flow diagrams
- Error handling procedures
- Security considerations
- Usage examples"

Better documentation makes your software more maintainable and accessible to new team members.

By aligning AI-assisted development with user-centric principles, establishing effective feedback loops, incorporating behavioral data, and pursuing iterative improvements, you can build software that truly serves its users. Vibe coding isn't just about producing code quickly—it's about creating better solutions through a more responsive, data-informed development process.

In the next chapter, we'll explore techniques for debugging and refining projects created through vibe coding.

Chapter 9: Debugging and Refining Vibe-Coded Projects

Even with AI assistance, debugging and refining code remains an essential part of the development process. While AI tools can generate functional code quickly, they don't eliminate the need for troubleshooting and optimization. This chapter explores techniques for effectively debugging AI-generated code and refining your projects to production quality.

Techniques for Debugging AI-Generated Code

Debugging code written with AI assistance presents unique challenges. The code might use approaches you wouldn't have chosen yourself, or implement patterns you're less familiar with. These techniques will help you navigate these challenges.

Understanding Before Debugging

Before attempting to fix issues, make sure you understand how the code works:

1. Ask the AI to explain the code's logic and structure

2. Identify the main components and their relationships
3. Trace the data flow through the system
4. Recognize the design patterns being used

This understanding provides the foundation for effective debugging.

Isolation Testing

Break down complex AI-generated functions into testable units:

1. Extract smaller functions from large blocks of code
2. Create test cases for each isolated component
3. Verify that each piece works as expected independently
4. Recombine components once they're working correctly

This divide-and-conquer approach makes complex problems more manageable.

Strategic Logging

Add logging at key points to track execution flow:

```
function processUserData(userData) {
```

```
  console.log('Starting processing with:', userData);

  // Data validation
  if (!userData.email) {
    console.log('Validation failed: missing email');
    return { success: false, error: 'Email required' };
  }

  // Processing steps
  const normalizedData =
normalizeUserInput(userData);
  console.log('After normalization:', normalizedData);

  const result = saveToDatabase(normalizedData);
  console.log('Database save result:', result);

  return result;
}
```

These logs create breadcrumbs that help you follow the execution path and identify where things go wrong.

Comparative Debugging

When facing persistent issues, create a simplified version:

1. Implement a basic version of the functionality manually
2. Compare behavior between your version and the AI-generated code
3. Identify differences in approach or output
4. Use these insights to locate the source of problems

This comparison often reveals subtle issues that might otherwise be hard to spot.

Leveraging AI for Debugging

Use AI tools to help debug their own output:

"This function for processing user payments occasionally fails with the error 'Cannot read property 'amount' of undefined'. Here's the code:

```
function processPayment(order) {
  const tax = calculateTax(order.items);
  const total = order.items.reduce((sum, item) =>
sum + item.price * item.quantity, 0);
  return chargeCustomer(order.customer.id, total +
tax);
}
```

What might be causing this error and how can I fix it?"

AI tools can often identify potential issues in code they've generated.

Identifying Common Patterns of Errors

AI-generated code tends to exhibit certain types of errors more frequently than others. Recognizing these patterns helps you spot and fix issues more quickly.

Assumption Errors

AI tools often make assumptions about the environment or available resources:

- Assuming browser APIs are available in Node.js environments
- Expecting certain libraries or dependencies to be installed
- Presuming specific browser features are supported
- Assuming file system access is available

Check for these assumption mismatches when code fails in your specific environment.

Edge Case Oversights

AI-generated code typically handles the happy path well but may miss edge cases:

- Empty arrays or objects
- Null or undefined values
- Extremely large or small numbers
- Unicode characters or special strings
- Concurrent operations

Explicitly test these edge cases to identify potential issues.

Context Misunderstandings

AI might misinterpret the context of your request:

- Generating frontend code when you needed backend functionality
- Creating synchronous code when asynchronous was required
- Implementing a solution for the wrong programming paradigm
- Misunderstanding domain-specific terminology

These misalignments often require restructuring rather than simple fixes.

Outdated Patterns

AI models trained on older codebases might generate outdated approaches:

- Using deprecated APIs or methods
- Implementing security practices that are no longer recommended
- Following patterns that don't align with current best practices
- Missing newer, more efficient approaches

Stay alert for these outdated patterns, especially in rapidly evolving technologies.

Inconsistent Naming and Styling

AI-generated code might mix different naming conventions or styling approaches:

- Mixing camelCase and snake_case
- Inconsistent function naming patterns
- Varying indentation or formatting
- Mixed quote styles or other syntax preferences

While these issues don't affect functionality, they impact readability and maintenance.

Working Around AI Limitations

When you encounter limitations in what AI can generate, several strategies can help you work around these constraints.

Hybrid Implementation Approach

Combine AI-generated code with manual implementation:

1. Use AI to generate the structure and boilerplate
2. Manually implement complex business logic
3. Use AI again to help with testing and documentation
4. Review and refine the combined solution

This hybrid approach leverages AI strengths while compensating for its limitations.

Progressive Enhancement

Start with a simple implementation and progressively add complexity:

1. Ask for a basic version that handles the core functionality
2. Test and verify this foundation works correctly
3. Gradually request enhancements for specific aspects

4. Integrate these enhancements into the main codebase

This step-by-step approach prevents overwhelming the AI with complex requirements.

Template and Customize

Use AI-generated code as a starting template:

1. Generate a solution that's close to what you need
2. Identify parts that require customization
3. Modify these sections to meet your specific requirements
4. Verify the customized solution works as expected

This approach gives you a head start while allowing for necessary adjustments.

Component Assembly

Break complex systems into manageable components:

1. Define clear interfaces between components
2. Generate each component separately
3. Manually integrate the components

4. Test the integrated system

This modular approach makes it easier for AI to generate high-quality code for each piece.

Testing for Performance, Security, and Reliability

Thorough testing is essential for refining AI-generated code to production quality.

Performance Testing

Evaluate and optimize the efficiency of AI-generated code:

1. Establish performance baselines and targets
2. Test with realistic data volumes and usage patterns
3. Identify bottlenecks using profiling tools
4. Request optimizations for problematic areas
5. Verify improvements with repeated testing

This systematic approach ensures your code meets performance requirements.

Security Assessment

Carefully evaluate security aspects of AI-generated code:

1. Review input validation and sanitization
2. Check for proper authentication and authorization
3. Examine data protection measures
4. Test for common vulnerabilities (injection attacks, XSS, CSRF)
5. Verify secure communication and data storage

These security checks help prevent vulnerabilities that might not be apparent from functional testing.

Reliability Testing

Ensure your code works consistently under various conditions:

1. Test with different input combinations
2. Simulate resource constraints (memory, CPU, network)
3. Introduce artificial delays and failures
4. Verify proper error handling and recovery
5. Test concurrent operations and race conditions

This reliability testing helps create robust applications that handle real-world conditions.

Automated Testing Implementation

Ask AI to help create comprehensive test suites:

"Generate unit tests for this user authentication module. Include tests for:

- Successful login and registration flows
- Invalid credentials handling
- Password reset functionality
- Account lockout after failed attempts
- Session management and timeout handling"

These automated tests provide ongoing verification as you continue to refine your code.

Refining Prompts to Improve Code Quality

As you gain experience with vibe coding, you'll learn to craft prompts that produce higher-quality code from the start.

Specificity in Requirements

Be explicit about quality requirements:

"Create a function to process user uploads that:

- Validates file types and sizes before processing
- Handles errors gracefully with informative messages
- Includes proper logging for debugging

- Uses memory efficiently for large files
- Follows the repository pattern for storage operations"

These specific requirements guide the AI toward higher-quality implementations.

Example-Driven Prompts

Provide examples that demonstrate your quality standards:

"Here's an example of a well-structured component in our codebase:

// Example of high-quality code

Please follow similar patterns for error handling, commenting, and structure when creating the new payment processing component."

These examples communicate your expectations more clearly than abstract guidelines.

Iterative Prompt Refinement

Treat prompt writing as an iterative process:

1. Start with a basic prompt
2. Evaluate the generated code

3. Identify quality issues or misalignments
4. Refine your prompt to address these specific issues
5. Generate a new version and reassess

This refinement cycle helps you develop more effective prompting techniques over time.

Quality-Focused Follow-ups

Use follow-up prompts that focus on specific quality aspects:

"The basic functionality looks good. Now let's improve:

1. Can you add comprehensive error handling?
2. Please optimize the database queries for better performance.
3. Add detailed comments explaining the more complex sections.
4. Implement proper input validation for all user-provided data."

These targeted follow-ups help refine the code in stages.

By applying these debugging and refinement techniques, you can transform AI-generated code from a rough draft into production-quality software. The combination of systematic debugging, thorough testing, and refined prompting creates a powerful workflow for developing robust applications with AI assistance.

In the next chapter, we'll explore real-world applications of vibe coding across different project types and scales.

Chapter 10: Real-World Applications of Vibe Coding

Vibe coding isn't just a theoretical concept—it's a practical approach that's changing how real projects get built. This chapter explores concrete applications of AI-assisted programming across different project types and scales, helping you identify where this approach can add the most value in your own work.

Prototyping Small Projects like Apps, Games, and Utilities

Small projects offer perfect opportunities to leverage vibe coding, allowing rapid development with minimal setup.

Mobile App Prototyping

AI tools excel at generating the foundational elements of mobile apps:

"Create a React Native component for a fitness tracking app's main dashboard. It should display:

- Daily step count with a circular progress indicator
- Weekly activity summary as a bar chart

- Recent workouts in a scrollable list
- Quick action buttons for starting new activities"

This prompt might generate a functional component that you can immediately integrate into your prototype, saving hours of implementation time.

The real advantage comes when iterating on designs:

"Users found the dashboard cluttered. Let's simplify by:

- Moving the weekly summary to a separate tab
- Enlarging the daily progress indicator
- Limiting the recent workouts list to three items
- Adding a 'See More' button for additional workouts"

These rapid iterations allow you to test multiple designs quickly, finding the best solution through experimentation rather than speculation.

Game Development Acceleration

Game prototypes benefit from AI assistance with both logic and assets:

"Generate a JavaScript function for a 2D platformer game's character controller. It should handle:

- Left/right movement with appropriate acceleration and deceleration
- Jumping with variable height based on button press duration
- Wall sliding and wall jumping
- Ground detection and platform interaction"

This core gameplay code gives you a starting point that you can tune to achieve the right feel.

For game mechanics, AI can help explore creative variations:

"I'm creating a card game where players build energy networks. Generate three different scoring mechanisms that would encourage different strategic approaches."

This creative input helps you explore design spaces more efficiently than brainstorming alone.

Utility Tool Creation

Productivity tools and utilities come together quickly with AI assistance:

"Create a Python script that monitors a folder for new image files and automatically:

- Resizes them to standard dimensions
- Optimizes them for web use
- Renames them according to a consistent pattern
- Generates appropriate metadata"

Such utilities might take only minutes to generate with AI but save hours of repetitive work when used.

The key advantage for utility development is handling edge cases:

"The image processing script works well, but needs to handle these additional scenarios:

- Corrupt or incomplete image files
- Files that are already optimized
- Very large images that might cause memory issues
- Various image formats including RAW files"

This comprehensive error handling makes utilities robust enough for real-world use.

Scaling Vibe Coding to Mid-Level Systems

As projects grow in complexity, vibe coding requires more structure but continues to offer significant benefits.

Web Application Development

Mid-sized web applications benefit from component-based AI assistance:

"I'm building an e-commerce platform with React and Node.js. Generate the product listing component that:

- Displays products in a responsive grid
- Includes filtering by category, price, and ratings
- Supports sorting by different criteria
- Implements lazy loading for performance
- Includes accessibility features for screen readers"

By generating components with clear boundaries, you can assemble complex applications while maintaining architectural control.

The backend benefits similarly from modular generation:

"Create an Express.js API endpoint for product search that:

- Accepts query parameters for filters and sorting
- Implements pagination for large result sets
- Optimizes database queries for performance
- Includes proper error handling
- Returns results in a consistent JSON format"

These generated components work together within your overall architecture.

Data Processing Pipelines

Data-intensive applications leverage AI for processing logic:

"Generate a Python function that processes customer transaction data to:

- Identify unusual spending patterns
- Group purchases into categories
- Calculate monthly spending trends
- Flag potentially fraudulent transactions"

This analytical logic might be tedious to write manually but can be quickly generated and then refined with AI assistance.

The pipeline approach works well with vibe coding:

"I need a data pipeline with these stages:

1. Data extraction from multiple sources
2. Cleaning and normalization
3. Feature engineering for machine learning
4. Model training and evaluation
5. Results visualization

Let's start with the extraction stage for these three data sources..."

Breaking the system into stages makes complex pipelines manageable with AI assistance.

Content Management Systems

Custom CMS development benefits from AI-generated components:

"Create a content editing interface that supports:

- Rich text editing with formatting options
- Image and media embedding
- Version history and comparison
- Collaborative editing with presence indicators
- Preview functionality for different device sizes"

These complex interfaces come together more quickly with AI-generated starting points.

The modular nature of CMS systems aligns well with vibe coding:

"Generate the schema and CRUD operations for these content types:

1. Articles with categories, tags, and related content
2. Product pages with specifications, pricing, and inventory
3. Team member profiles with roles, bios, and contact information"

Each module can be generated, tested, and integrated independently.

When and Where Vibe Coding Works Best

Understanding the sweet spots for AI-assisted programming helps you apply it where it adds the most value.

Ideal Project Characteristics

Vibe coding provides the greatest benefits for projects with these traits:

Well-defined components: Systems that can be broken into clear, somewhat independent parts allow you to generate each component separately.

Standard patterns: Projects following established patterns (CRUD applications, RESTful APIs, etc.) benefit from AI's knowledge of these common approaches.

Iterative development: Projects where you expect multiple rounds of feedback and refinement leverage the rapid iteration capabilities of AI assistance.

Balanced complexity: Problems complex enough to be time-consuming but not so novel that they require groundbreaking approaches work best with current AI tools.

Documentation needs: Projects requiring extensive documentation benefit from AI's ability to generate explanations and examples alongside code.

Ideal Development Phases

Certain development phases benefit more from AI assistance:

Initial prototyping: When exploring concepts and validating ideas, AI's speed helps you test multiple approaches quickly.

Boilerplate creation: Setting up project foundations, configuration, and standard components accelerates with AI assistance.

Feature expansion: Adding new capabilities to existing systems works well when AI can understand the current codebase.

Refactoring: Updating code to new patterns or technologies benefits from AI's knowledge of different implementation styles.

Documentation: Creating user guides, API documentation, and internal references becomes more efficient with AI help.

Less Suitable Scenarios

Some situations benefit less from current AI coding tools:

Highly innovative algorithms: Truly novel approaches might require human creativity and deep domain expertise.

Safety-critical systems: Applications where failures could cause harm need extensive human verification, potentially reducing the efficiency benefits.

Extremely performance-sensitive code: Low-level optimizations often require human understanding of hardware and execution details.

Highly specialized domains: Niche fields with limited public code examples might challenge AI tools trained on more common codebases.

Legacy system maintenance: Very old systems using obsolete technologies might fall outside the AI's training data.

Avoiding Missteps While Adopting Vibe Coding in Professional Environments

Introducing AI-assisted programming in professional settings requires careful consideration to avoid potential pitfalls.

Transparent Communication

Be open about AI usage with stakeholders:

- Explain how AI tools fit into your development process

- Clarify that AI assists rather than replaces human judgment
- Share examples of how AI improves productivity and quality
- Address concerns about code ownership and security

This transparency builds trust and sets appropriate expectations.

Gradual Integration

Introduce vibe coding incrementally:

1. Start with low-risk, internal tools or prototypes
2. Establish clear guidelines for AI usage
3. Train team members on effective prompting techniques
4. Gradually expand to more critical components as confidence grows

This measured approach allows teams to adapt comfortably to new workflows.

Quality Control Processes

Establish clear processes for verifying AI-generated code:

- Create review checklists specific to AI-generated components
- Implement automated testing requirements
- Define security review procedures
- Establish performance benchmarks that must be met

These guardrails ensure that productivity gains don't come at the expense of quality.

Knowledge Sharing

Foster a culture of learning around AI tools:

- Document effective prompting strategies
- Share successful AI collaboration patterns
- Create libraries of validated, reusable components
- Discuss challenges and solutions openly

This knowledge sharing helps the entire team benefit from individual discoveries.

Ethical Considerations

Address ethical aspects of AI code generation:

- Review licensing implications of AI-generated code
- Consider attribution and transparency in documentation
- Establish policies for sensitive or regulated code
- Discuss potential biases in AI suggestions

These considerations help navigate the evolving ethical landscape of AI-assisted development.

By understanding where vibe coding works best and how to integrate it responsibly into professional environments, you can maximize its benefits while avoiding potential problems. The most successful implementations treat AI as a team member with specific strengths and limitations, integrated thoughtfully into existing development processes.

In the next chapter, we'll explore best practices for sustainable vibe coding that maintains quality and developer growth over the long term.

Chapter 11: Best Practices for Sustainable Vibe Coding

As AI-assisted programming becomes a regular part of your workflow, establishing sustainable practices ensures long-term success. This chapter explores how to balance the immediate productivity gains of vibe coding with the need for maintainable code, continuous learning, and team collaboration.

Balancing AI Speed with Manual Precision

The speed of AI-generated code can be seductive, but balancing this speed with careful human oversight creates the best results.

Defining Quality Thresholds

Establish clear standards for when code is ready for production:

- Create a checklist of quality criteria that all code must meet
- Define which aspects require manual review versus automated checks
- Set different thresholds for different types of components based on criticality

- Document these standards so all team members share the same expectations

These thresholds help you decide when to accept AI-generated code and when to refine it further.

Time-Quality Trade-off Framework

Develop a framework for making conscious trade-off decisions:

Context	Speed Priority	Quality Priority
Prototyping	Higher	Lower
Core features	Lower	Higher
Internal tools	Higher	Moderate
Customer-facing	Moderate	Higher
Security-related	Lowest	Highest

This framework helps you apply appropriate standards to different situations.

Strategic Manual Intervention

Identify where human attention adds the most value:

- Architecture and system design decisions
- Security-sensitive components
- Performance-critical sections
- Complex business logic
- User experience flows

Focus your manual efforts on these high-impact areas while leveraging AI for more routine aspects.

Continuous Validation

Implement ongoing validation processes:

- Automated tests that verify both functionality and quality standards
- Regular code reviews that include AI-generated components
- Performance monitoring to catch degradation
- User feedback collection to identify experience issues

This continuous validation catches issues that might slip through initial reviews.

Setting Standards for Maintainable AI-Generated Code

Maintainability becomes particularly important for AI-generated code, which might use approaches different from your usual patterns.

Documentation Requirements

Establish strong documentation practices:

- Require comments explaining the purpose and approach of AI-generated functions
- Document assumptions and limitations explicitly
- Create usage examples for complex components
- Maintain a record of which parts were AI-generated for future reference

This documentation helps future developers understand the code, regardless of its origin.

Consistency Guidelines

Create guidelines for maintaining consistency:

- Define naming conventions that AI-generated code must follow

- Establish project-specific patterns for common operations
- Create templates for standard components
- Document the preferred architectural approach for your project

Share these guidelines in your prompts to help AI generate more consistent code.

Refactoring Criteria

Define when AI-generated code should be refactored:

- When it doesn't follow your established patterns
- When it's difficult to understand or modify
- When it contains duplicated logic that could be consolidated
- When it uses outdated or inefficient approaches
- When it doesn't meet performance requirements

These criteria help you identify code that needs improvement despite being functionally correct.

Maintainability Reviews

Implement specific reviews focused on maintainability:

- Ask team members not involved in the original development to review for clarity
- Consider how the code would be modified for likely future requirements
- Evaluate how easily new team members could understand the code
- Check for appropriate abstraction and separation of concerns

These focused reviews help catch maintainability issues early.

Collaborating with Teams on AI-Assisted Workflows

As vibe coding extends beyond individual use to team environments, effective collaboration becomes essential.

Shared Prompt Libraries

Create team resources for effective AI interaction:

- Maintain a collection of proven prompts for common tasks

- Document which prompting approaches work best for different situations
- Share examples of particularly successful AI collaborations
- Update these resources as you discover better techniques

These shared resources help the entire team benefit from individual learning.

Code Review Adaptations

Adjust code review processes for AI-generated components:

- Focus reviews on architectural alignment and business logic correctness
- Ask authors to highlight which parts were AI-generated versus manually written
- Look for inconsistencies between AI-generated and human-written sections
- Pay special attention to security and edge case handling

These adaptations help reviewers focus on the most important aspects.

Knowledge Sharing Sessions

Establish regular opportunities to share AI collaboration techniques:

- Hold workshops on effective prompting strategies
- Discuss challenging problems and how AI helped (or didn't help) solve them
- Share before-and-after examples of refined AI-generated code
- Explore new AI tools and capabilities as they emerge

These sessions spread knowledge and build team capability.

Clear Responsibility Guidelines

Define who's responsible for different aspects of AI-generated code:

- The developer who prompted and integrated the code owns its quality
- Reviewers verify adherence to team standards
- Everyone shares responsibility for identifying potential improvements
- Leadership establishes appropriate usage policies

These clear responsibilities prevent quality issues from falling through the cracks.

Continuous Learning: Staying Adaptable in a Fast-Changing Landscape

The field of AI-assisted programming evolves rapidly. Maintaining a learning mindset helps you adapt to these changes.

Deliberate Skill Preservation

Actively maintain your core programming skills:

- Regularly solve problems without AI assistance
- Understand the code AI generates rather than just using it
- Practice explaining and teaching programming concepts
- Stay current with language features and best practices

These habits prevent over-dependence on AI tools.

Experimental Learning Projects

Create space for exploration and learning:

- Dedicate time to try new AI tools and techniques
- Experiment with different prompting approaches
- Build small projects using unfamiliar technologies with AI assistance
- Compare different AI tools on the same tasks

These experiments expand your capabilities and understanding.

Feedback Analysis

Learn from your interactions with AI tools:

- Note which types of requests produce the best results
- Identify patterns in areas where AI consistently falls short
- Analyze how changes in your prompting affect the output
- Track how AI capabilities evolve over time

This analysis helps you use AI tools more effectively.

Community Engagement

Connect with the broader vibe coding community:

- Participate in forums and discussions about AI-assisted development
- Share your experiences and learn from others
- Follow researchers and practitioners in the field
- Contribute to open-source projects that use or enhance AI coding tools

This engagement keeps you informed about emerging practices and tools.

Balanced Skill Development

Focus your learning on areas that complement AI capabilities:

- System architecture and design
- Problem decomposition and analysis
- User experience and human factors
- Ethical considerations in software development
- Communication and collaboration skills

These areas enhance your ability to guide AI effectively while developing skills AI doesn't possess.

By implementing these best practices, you create a sustainable approach to vibe coding that balances immediate productivity with long-term code quality and professional growth. The most successful practitioners view AI as a partner in the development process—one with specific strengths and limitations—rather than a replacement for human skills and judgment.

In the next chapter, we'll explore the ethical dimensions of AI-assisted programming and how to approach this powerful technology responsibly.

Chapter 12: Ethics and Responsibility in Vibe Coding

As AI-assisted programming becomes more prevalent, ethical considerations take on increasing importance. The power to generate code quickly brings responsibilities regarding its quality, impact, and appropriate use. This chapter explores the ethical dimensions of vibe coding and how to approach this technology responsibly.

Accountability in AI-Assisted Programming

When code is generated with AI assistance, questions of accountability naturally arise. Who is responsible when something goes wrong?

The Developer's Responsibility

As a developer using AI tools, you retain primary responsibility for the code you deploy:

- You choose to accept, modify, or reject AI suggestions
- You decide which components to generate with AI assistance

- You determine when code is ready for production
- You select the contexts where AI-generated code is appropriate

This responsibility requires maintaining sufficient understanding of the code to evaluate its correctness and implications.

Establishing Clear Ownership

Create explicit policies regarding code ownership:

- Document which parts of your codebase were created with AI assistance
- Establish that all code, regardless of origin, falls under your organization's responsibility
- Define review and approval processes for AI-generated components
- Create audit trails that track the evolution of code from initial generation through refinement

These policies help clarify accountability both internally and externally.

Transparency with Stakeholders

Be open with stakeholders about your use of AI tools:

- Inform clients or users when appropriate
- Explain how AI assists your development process
- Clarify that AI tools augment rather than replace human judgment
- Address concerns about quality, security, or other implications

This transparency builds trust and sets appropriate expectations.

Legal and Licensing Considerations

Stay informed about the evolving legal landscape:

- Understand the licensing terms of AI tools you use
- Consider intellectual property implications of AI-generated code
- Stay current with regulations that might affect AI use in your industry
- Consult legal experts when working in regulated domains

These legal considerations help you navigate an area where standards are still developing.

Addressing Biases in AI-Generated Code

AI systems reflect biases present in their training data, which can manifest in the code they generate. Recognizing and addressing these biases is an ethical imperative.

Types of Bias in Code Generation

Be aware of how bias might appear in AI-generated code:

- **Representation bias**: Favoring approaches common in training data while overlooking alternatives
- **Terminology bias**: Using naming conventions that reflect cultural or gender biases
- **Accessibility bias**: Generating code that works well for typical users but creates barriers for others
- **Security bias**: Implementing stronger protections for common use cases while leaving edge cases vulnerable

- **Documentation bias**: Explaining code in ways that assume certain background knowledge

These biases can subtly influence your codebase if not actively addressed.

Bias Detection Strategies

Implement processes to identify potential biases:

- Review variable and function names for inclusive language
- Test with diverse user scenarios and personas
- Examine security measures across different use contexts
- Have team members with varied backgrounds review code
- Check documentation for assumptions about user knowledge

These reviews help catch biases that might otherwise go unnoticed.

Mitigation Approaches

When biases are identified, take active steps to address them:

- Provide explicit guidance in your prompts about inclusive approaches
- Refine AI-generated code to remove biased elements
- Create templates and examples that demonstrate unbiased alternatives
- Establish team standards for reviewing code through an equity lens
- Share learnings about identified biases to raise awareness

These mitigation strategies help create more equitable and inclusive code.

Continuous Improvement

Treat bias mitigation as an ongoing process:

- Stay informed about evolving best practices for inclusive coding
- Regularly review and update your guidance for AI tools
- Collect feedback from diverse users and team members
- Adjust your processes as you learn more about potential biases

This continuous improvement helps address both known and emerging bias concerns.

Avoiding Over-Dependence on AI Tools

While AI coding assistants offer powerful capabilities, becoming overly dependent on them carries risks for both individual developers and organizations.

Signs of Unhealthy Dependence

Watch for these warning signs:

- Difficulty writing simple functions without AI assistance
- Decreasing understanding of how your code actually works
- Reduced ability to debug issues in AI-generated code
- Discomfort when AI tools are temporarily unavailable
- Declining interest in learning new programming concepts

These signs suggest an imbalance that could affect long-term capabilities.

Maintaining Core Skills

Actively preserve your fundamental programming abilities:

- Regularly write code without AI assistance
- Challenge yourself to understand every line of AI-generated code
- Practice explaining how complex functions work
- Solve programming puzzles that exercise core concepts
- Stay current with language features and paradigms

These habits keep your skills sharp even as you leverage AI for productivity.

Balanced Learning Approaches

Use AI as a learning accelerator rather than a replacement for understanding:

- Ask AI to explain concepts you don't fully grasp
- Generate multiple solutions and analyze the differences
- Use AI-generated code as a starting point for deeper exploration

- Challenge yourself to improve upon AI suggestions
- Study patterns in AI-generated code to expand your knowledge

This learning-focused approach turns AI into a teaching tool rather than a crutch.

Organizational Safeguards

Implement team practices that prevent over-dependence:

- Rotate responsibilities so everyone maintains diverse skills
- Hold code reviews that focus on understanding, not just functionality
- Create learning opportunities that develop fundamental abilities
- Establish coding exercises that don't involve AI assistance
- Prepare contingency plans for situations where AI tools are unavailable

These safeguards help maintain team capabilities regardless of tool availability.

Ensuring Transparency in AI-Coding Workflows

Transparency about how AI tools are used builds
trust with team members, stakeholders, and users.

Documentation Practices

Establish clear documentation about AI usage:

- Note which components were created with AI
  assistance
- Document the prompting strategies used for
  critical code
- Explain why AI was appropriate for specific
  components
- Record any limitations or concerns with
  AI-generated sections

This documentation helps future maintainers
understand the code's origins.

Communication Guidelines

Create standards for discussing AI contributions:

- Be honest about the role of AI in your
  development process
- Avoid attributing creativity or understanding to
  AI tools

- Clarify that human judgment guides all AI usage
- Explain how AI-generated code is verified and tested

These communication practices prevent misunderstandings about how code is created.

Audit Trails

Maintain records of AI interactions for important code:

- Save prompts used to generate critical components
- Document iterations and refinements of AI-generated code
- Track which team members reviewed and approved AI contributions
- Note any issues discovered and how they were addressed

These audit trails provide accountability and help improve future processes.

User Awareness

Consider when and how to inform users about AI-generated components:

- In medical, financial, or safety-critical applications, transparency may be ethically required
- For general applications, focus on outcomes and quality rather than creation methods
- When AI generates user-facing text or designs, consider appropriate disclosure
- Follow emerging best practices and regulations in your industry

This thoughtful approach to user awareness respects their right to relevant information.

By addressing these ethical considerations, you can use AI coding tools responsibly while maintaining professional integrity. The most ethical approach views AI as a powerful tool whose use requires careful judgment, ongoing learning, and a commitment to creating software that serves users well.

As vibe coding continues to evolve, the ethical frameworks surrounding it will develop too. Staying engaged with these discussions and contributing your experiences helps shape practices that maximize benefits while minimizing potential harms.

In our final chapter, we'll reflect on the future of programming in an AI-assisted world and how developers can thrive in this changing landscape.

My Final Word On The Future of Programming

As we reach the end of our exploration into vibe coding, it's worth reflecting on what this shift means for the future of programming and for you as a developer. The integration of AI into the coding process represents more than just a new tool—it signals a fundamental evolution in how we create software.

The Changing Nature of Programming

Programming has always evolved. From assembly language to compiled languages, from procedural to object-oriented paradigms, from monolithic applications to microservices—each shift has changed what it means to be a programmer. The rise of AI-assisted coding represents the next major evolution in this journey.

This change doesn't make programming easier so much as it changes what we focus on. Rather than spending hours on syntax and boilerplate code, developers now concentrate more on problem definition, architecture, and quality assessment. The mechanical aspects of coding diminish in importance while the creative and evaluative aspects grow.

This shift mirrors what happened when calculators became widespread. Mathematicians didn't become obsolete—they simply focused less on computation and more on problem-solving and proof development. Similarly, programmers aren't becoming obsolete; they're evolving to focus on higher-level concerns while partnering with AI for implementation details.

Core Principles for Successful Vibe Coding

Throughout this book, we've explored many techniques and approaches for effective AI-assisted programming. These can be distilled into several core principles:

Maintain ownership and understanding. Never cede your responsibility to understand the code in your projects. Use AI as a collaborator, not a replacement for your judgment.

Focus on clear communication. Your ability to communicate clearly with AI tools—through well-crafted prompts and iterative feedback—largely determines your success with vibe coding.

Preserve your fundamental skills. Continue to develop your programming knowledge and problem-solving abilities. These foundational skills make you a better partner for AI tools.

Embrace iterative refinement. Accept that AI-generated code is often a starting point rather than a finished product. Build your workflow around progressive improvement.

Balance speed with quality. Use the productivity gains from AI assistance thoughtfully, investing some of that saved time into deeper review and refinement.

Stay adaptable and curious. The field of AI-assisted development is evolving rapidly. Maintain a learning mindset and explore new capabilities as they emerge.

These principles will serve you well regardless of how AI tools evolve in the coming years.

The Evolving Relationship Between Human Developers and AI

The relationship between developers and AI tools will continue to evolve. Today's experience of providing prompts and receiving code suggestions represents just the beginning of this partnership.

We're likely to see more interactive collaboration, with AI tools that can participate in design discussions, suggest architectural approaches, identify potential issues before coding begins, and learn your preferences over time. The line between human and AI contributions may blur as these tools become more deeply integrated into the development process.

This evolution will bring both opportunities and challenges. The opportunities include greater productivity, more accessible software development, and the ability to tackle more complex problems. The challenges involve maintaining human skills, ensuring code quality, and navigating the ethical implications of increasingly capable AI systems.

Your role in this evolving relationship is active, not passive. How you choose to use AI tools, what skills you develop, and what standards you uphold will shape not just your personal experience but the broader development of AI-assisted programming.

The Human Element Remains Essential

Despite the impressive capabilities of AI coding assistants, the human element in programming remains irreplaceable. Only human developers can:

Understand the true needs of users. AI can generate code based on specifications, but only humans can empathize with users and translate their unstated needs into software requirements.

Make ethical judgments. Decisions about privacy, security, accessibility, and fairness require human values and judgment that AI systems don't possess.

Provide creative vision. The most innovative software solutions come from human creativity, intuition, and the ability to make unexpected connections.

Take responsibility. Accountability for software and its impacts ultimately rests with the humans who create and deploy it, not with the tools they use.

Find meaning in the work. The satisfaction of solving problems and creating useful software is a uniquely human experience that gives purpose to our professional lives.

These human contributions ensure that programming remains a creative, meaningful profession even as the mechanical aspects become increasingly automated.

An Invitation to Explore

As we conclude this book, I invite you to approach vibe coding with a spirit of exploration. This field is still in its early stages, with new tools, techniques, and best practices emerging regularly. Your experiences and insights will help shape how AI-assisted programming develops.

Experiment with different approaches, share what you learn with others, and contribute to the growing body of knowledge about effective human-AI collaboration in software development. Be both enthusiastic about the possibilities and thoughtful about the implications.

Remember that you're not just a user of AI tools but a pioneer in a new approach to creating software. Your choices about how to integrate these tools into your work will influence not just your own productivity but the future direction of our field.

The most exciting aspect of vibe coding isn't the technology itself but the new possibilities it creates—the problems we can now solve, the software we can now build, and the creative potential we can now unlock. By combining human creativity and judgment with AI capabilities, we can create better software than either could produce alone.

The future of programming isn't about humans versus AI—it's about humans and AI working together to create software that improves lives. That future begins with you and the choices you make about how to apply these powerful new tools in your daily work.

Welcome to the age of vibe coding. The journey has just begun.

Disclaimer

This book is intended for educational purposes only.
While every effort has been made to ensure accuracy,
the author and publisher make no guarantees
regarding the completeness, reliability, or current
validity of the content. The programming examples
and AI tools referenced (such as Gemini, OpenAI,
and others) may change over time, and results may
vary depending on updates, user configurations, or
third-party API limitations.

The author assumes no responsibility for any errors
or omissions, or for any damages arising from the use
of the material. Readers are encouraged to consult
official documentation and terms of service for all
referenced tools and APIs. This book is not affiliated
with, endorsed by, or sponsored by any mentioned
platforms.

Use the information at your own risk and always test
responsibly.

ABOUT THE AUTHOR

Harrell Howard is a prolific author and thought leader, specializing in a diverse array of subjects that cater to both personal and professional development. With a deep passion for empowering readers through knowledge, Harrell has penned numerous best-selling books, each offering practical insights and actionable strategies across various fields.

Harrell Howard combines a rich background in technology, marketing, and personal development to deliver content that is both insightful and practical.

When he's not writing, Harrell enjoys exploring new tech, market trends, and sharing his knowledge via speaking engagements and workshops. His drive for lifelong learning & passion for helping others is evident in his book.